What I am about to
tell you IS NOT to
leave this room...

The Corps has developed a new CODE BASED ON THE NAVAJO LANGUAGE that could very well win this war...

There are ONLY A FEW MEN IN THIS WORLD who can speak this code...

Your mission is to
KEEP YOUR CODE
TALKER ALIVE...

...but should he fall into enemy hands, your mission is to PROTECT THE CODE AT ALL COSTS.

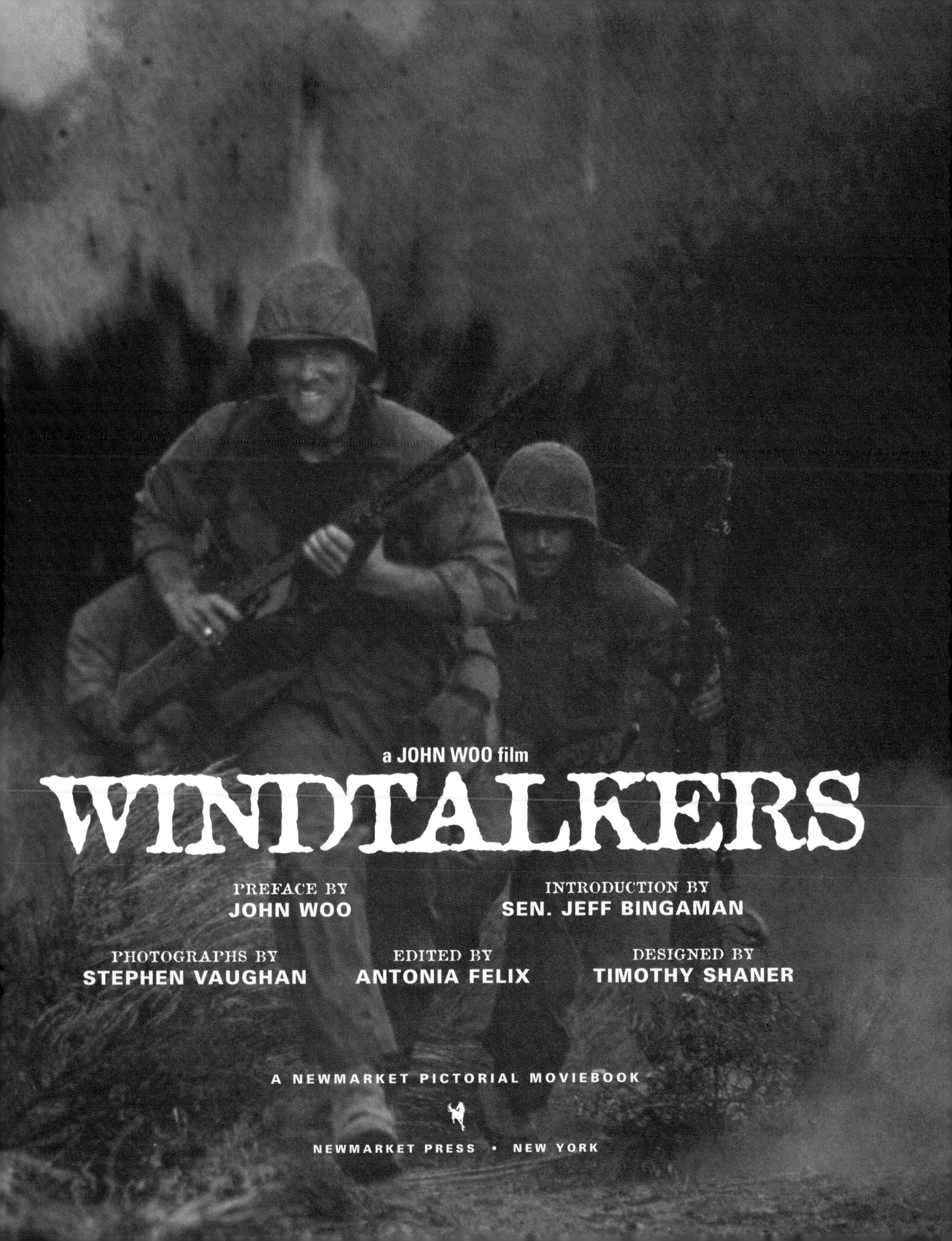

a JOHN WOO film

WINDTALKERS

PREFACE BY
JOHN WOO

INTRODUCTION BY
SEN. JEFF BINGAMAN

PHOTOGRAPHS BY
STEPHEN VAUGHAN

EDITED BY
ANTONIA FELIX

DESIGNED BY
TIMOTHY SHANER

A NEWMARKET PICTORIAL MOVIEBOOK

NEWMARKET PRESS • NEW YORK

Screenplay and photographs from *Windtalkers* © 2002
Metro-Goldwyn-Mayer Studios, Inc. All rights reserved.

Acknowledgment of photographs and permission to reprint
copyrighted material appears on page 128.

This book is published in the United States of America.

First Edition

10 9 8 7 6 5 4 3 2 1

Library of Congress Cataloging-in-Publication Data
available upon request.

ISBN 1-55704-515-1

Design by Timothy Shaner.

Manufactured in the United States of America.

CONTENTS

PREFACE

BY JOHN WOO, DIRECTOR

ONE of the themes I have enjoyed portraying the most in my films is that of the code of honor. Whether it applies to family, friendship, honor among thieves, or the bond among soldiers, I believe that honor is one of our most compelling human traits. Films that focus on a challenge to personal honor make great storytelling—and when the story is based on real events, it brings the drama to a whole new level.

When I first heard the brief pitch for *Windtalkers*, I knew that it was a film I had to make. Here was a tale of personal honor, with Navajo men committing themselves to a top-secret program that only they can fulfill, and of military honor, with Marines forced to follow orders to protect this top-secret code above all else—even if it means taking the life of a fellow Marine.

The code talkers participated in every Pacific battle fought by the Marines from Guadalcanal in 1942 to Okinawa in 1945. The story of the Navajo code talkers of World War II is a tale of honor on many levels. It is also the story of bravery, patriotism, devotion to duty, and two different American cultures coming together for the first time.

As a person born in the East who lives and works in the West, I feel I have an opportunity to bridge some of the differences between those two cultures in my films. I have often found ways to express the challenges and rewards of bringing different types of people together. Two very different cultures meet for the first time in *Windtalkers*, even though they are both from the same country. Even though the Navajo who entered the military in World War II were American citizens, most of them lived on the Navajo Reservation in the southwest and had had little contact with the rest of the United States. The Marines they served with had never met Navajos before, and one of the duties of the "bodyguard" Marines was to protect the code talkers from being mistaken for Japanese by their own units. I think this is a very interesting situation—American soldiers were so unfamiliar with each other that they could mistake one of their own for the enemy. This also brings up the issue of prejudice, and how it is very easy to cut down people who come from a different background just because you don't know anything about them. All of these elements, and more, came through in my first meeting with the producers and screenwriters for *Windtalkers*.

Because we are dealing with a true, historical story, we wanted to get the blessing of the real code talkers for our film. I met several of them before we started shooting. We not only wanted to get their own personal experiences, but also their approval and support to make the movie. It made them happy to know that we wanted to make all the Marines heroes—not just the code talkers. It was very important to me to make everyone equally courageous. I am honored to have met code talkers such as Albert Smith, who worked closely with us as a consultant on the movie, as well as all the others who met with us and gave us their blessing.

On all my American projects, my producing partner, Terence Chang, and I work closely with the writers to sculpt the script. The code talker story allowed me to put a relationship drama—about the friendships that develop between the code talkers and the other Marines—within the context of war. Ten years earlier I wrote and directed another war movie, *Bullet in the Head*, about Vietnam. I wanted to show that war brings out the worst in people, not the best. But with *Windtalkers* I was given a story that shows something positive that comes out of war: friendship and personal transformation.

The stage of *Windtalkers* is the Battle of Saipan in 1944, a bloody and horrifying episode in the war in the Pacific. It is my hope that *Windtalkers* shows that war is, and always has been, the worst way to work out our differences. I also hope that it reveals that honor, such as that shown by the Navajo code talkers and everyone else who has served to protect their country, is one bright, shining thing that can come out of something as brutal and terrible as war.

This book takes an inside look at the making of *Windtalkers* and gives historical information about the Navajos and the code talker program. The code talkers have inspired me with their stories of bravery and skill and also with their beautiful and gentle philosophy of life. I am very happy to be able to bring their story to the world with *Windtalkers*. The film and this book are an affectionate testament to the code talkers and to all who served in World War II.

ABOVE: Director John Woo, right, with Director of Photography Jeffrey L. Kimball, center, on the set. OPPOSITE: Nicolas Cage as Sergeant Joe Enders.

PROFILE: JOHN WOO

JOHN Woo, hailed by the *Los Angeles Times* as "the best contemporary director of action films," made his U.S. feature film debut with *Hard Target* starring Jean-Claude Van Damme in 1992. He went on to direct the hits *Broken Arrow* with John Travolta and Christian Slater in 1995, *Face/Off* starring Travolta and Nicolas Cage in 1997, *Mission Impossible II* starring Tom Cruise in 2000, and *Windtalkers* in 2002.

Woo's career as a filmmaker began in Hong Kong where he spent more than two decades writing and directing greater than 26 feature films. He grew up in Hong Kong, but details of his early childhood there do little to foretell that he would become an internationally renowned movie director. "I was born in China in 1946, and after the communists took over we moved to Hong Kong in 1951," he said. "We were so poor that we could only afford to live in

ABOVE: Director John Woo, left, with actor Adam Beach.
OPPOSITE: Adam Beach as U.S. Marine code talker Yahzee.

a shack, and after the big fire of 1953 we became homeless. We lived on the street for years. After that we lived in a slum. The worst place in the world." Woo's father, a philosopher and scholar, could not get a job in Hong Kong and was struck down with tuberculosis. During the ten years that he was hospitalized, Mrs. Woo was left to raise John and his brother and sister alone. The family could not afford to send John to school, but with the help of a far-off family he was able to attend a school run by the Lutheran Church. "An American family sent us some money through the church and helped me to go to school for eight years," he said. "I am still very grateful to them." In spite of their poverty, John and his mother went to the movies often because tickets were cheap. "My mother was a big movie fan," he said, "and used to bring me to the theater. She was crazy about American movies: Clark Gable, Cary Grant. Even when I was in school I went to a movie almost every day. The first kinds of films I loved were French films and musicals—Gene Kelly and Fred Astaire and *West Side Story*."

At age 11, Woo began his first experiments with making movies by drawing scenes of cowboys, cartoon characters, and Chinese knights on glass and projecting them onto the wall with a flashlight and using a blanket as a projection booth. In his teen years he often skipped school to go to the movies, museums, and the library. "I followed art very much," he said, "and didn't care much about studying or homework." In high school he began acting and directing plays and knew that he had found his life's work. His father, however, had other plans for him. "He wanted me to carry on his study of Chinese culture," said Woo. "But he realized he couldn't change my mind, and before he died he said, 'You do whatever you want. Just keep straight and live with dignity.'"

In the 1960s, there was no film school in Hong Kong, and Woo's family could not afford to send him away to study. Instead, he learned film theory on his own through books and by watching and analyz-

"A director is not a dictator. A director gives people direction and is there to guide. And the actors sometimes will teach me about life."

—JOHN WOO

ing films with a group of young afficionados. They met in the offices of a newspaper, the *Chinese Student Weekly*. "The boss," said Woo, "was a very kind man; he made the office of the newspaper available as a sort of arts institute. There were several sections for poetry, art, philosophy, and I met a group of young people who loved film. The newspaper rented art films for us to watch."

Woo's first job in the industry was as a script supervisor at the Cathay Studio in Hong Kong. He then became an assistant for action-film director Chang Cheh at the Shaw Brothers studio. "He was a great master," Woo recalled, "and influenced the whole Hong Kong film industry." After working with Cheh for nearly two years, Woo worked as as an associate director with the popular TV comedian Michael Hui, who was making a transition to the big screen. In 1973, Woo set up a production company with a friend who had made a little money in the stock market and wanted to invest it. They created

Woo's directorial debut, *The Young Dragons*, a martial arts action movie with fight scenes choreographed by a young man who would soon evolve into one of Hong Kong's top stars: Jackie Chan.

Many of Woo's first films were comedies, but in the 1980s, he created a series of romantic and hard-hitting gangster dramas, such as *The Killer*, that broke box-office records. In 1993, he brought his talent and decades of experience to Hollywood and swiftly earned a reputation as a leading action film director, dubbed by one London paper as the "Mozart of mayhem."

For all its striking battle scenes, *Windtalkers* reveals perhaps more of Woo's vision as a filmmaker than any of his previous work. Filled with the action and explosive realities of war, *Windtalkers* is at heart a story about the human spirit. Actors who have worked with Woo have learned firsthand that he is an expert in that realm—and also a very accommodating boss. "A director is not a dictator," Woo said. "A director gives people direction and is there to guide. And the actors sometimes will teach me about life. All of mankind has the same kind of heart. Sometimes people are built in a different way but deep inside, basically everyone is the same. It's so nice to learn that."

The Films of John Woo

Windtalkers	2002	*The Time You Need A Friend*	1984
Mission Impossible II	2000	*The Sunset Warrior*	1983
Face/Off	1997	*Plain Jane to the Rescue*	1982
Broken Arrow	1995	*Laughing Times*	1981
Hard Target	1993	*From Riches to Rags*	1979
Hard Boiled	1992	*Last Hurrah for Chivalry*	1978
Once a Thief	1991	*Follow the Star*	1977
Bullet in the Head	1990	*Money Crazy*	1977
The Killer	1989	*Princess Cheung Ping*	1975
A Better Tomorrow II	1987	*Countdown in Kung Fu*	1975
A Better Tomorrow	1986	*The Dragon Tamers*	1974
Run Tiger Run	1985	*The Young Dragons*	1973

17

INTRODUCTION

BY SENATOR JEFF BINGAMAN

THE Navajo Nation is the largest Native American tribe in the Southwest, covering portions of Utah, Arizona, and my home state of New Mexico. As a U. S. senator from the "land of enchantment" for over 18 years, I've had the opportunity to travel around the state, speaking to numerous and varied groups on a dynamic and ever-changing range of issues and concerns. But one story always remained constant—an incredible tale of a group of World War II Navajo radio men who distinguished themselves in performing a unique, highly successful communications operation in the Pacific theater. These were the Navajo code talkers, whose very existence was shrouded in secrecy and who, at the conclusion of the war, dutifully stepped back into obscurity.

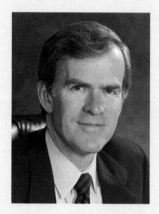

To truly appreciate how heroic the accomplishments of the code talkers were, we must also understand the cultural context in which they were operating. They experienced alienation in their own homeland and were discouraged from speaking their own language in schools. Yet they still stepped forward in defense of their country and developed the most significant and successful military code of the time. The code was so successful that military commanders credited it with saving the lives of countless American soldiers and significantly contributing to the successful engagements of the United States in the battles of Guadalcanal, Tarawa, Saipan, Iwo Jima, and Okinawa. But, while the bodies of their fallen comrades came home, simple messages of comfort to relatives back home on the reservations were prohibited by the very secrecy of the code's origin. At the end of the war, these unsung heroes returned to their homes on buses—no parades, no fanfare, no special recognition for what they had truly accomplished. Although the war was over, their duty—their oath of secrecy—continued. For the next 23 years, the Department of Defense maintained the code's sensitive classification, further obscuring the code talkers' achievements.

Even today, over 50 years later, many of these aging veterans talk only hesitantly about the past, often only when pressed for their stories. They proudly produce their service records, yellowed and crumbling with age, then carefully store them away once again, all the while claiming they did nothing out of the ordinary. But I disagree, as we all should recognize the true valor and commitment of these modest warriors. The Navajo code talkers are part of our nation's living heritage, the fabric that makes this country great.

In December 1999, I wrote to then Secretary of Defense William Cohen, asking the Department of Defense to review the code talkers' World War II military records and see what type of honors would be appropriate. Although they began almost immediately, I was informed it would take almost a year to complete the process. Military records of that time were incom-

ABOVE: New Mexico Senator Jeff Bingaman.
OPPOSITE: Native Americans (from left to right) Marine radio messengers PFC Joe Hosteen Kelwood of Steamboat Canyon, Canado, Arizona; Pvt. Floyd Saupitty of Lawton, Oklahoma (a Comanche); and PFC Alex Williams of Red Lake, Leupp, Arizona, on their way to Japanese war fronts in March 1945. Kelwood and Williams are Navajo.

plete and difficult to research, they told me, and it looked as if the very secrecy that protected the code now hampered efforts to reward its creators. To add to my dismay, it seemed almost every week I learned of another code talker's passing.

By early March 2000, after months of searching, one suggestion presented itself as a most fitting reward—Congressional Gold and Silver Medals. Of all the honors Congress can bestow, the awarding of Congressional Gold and Silver Medals is often considered the most distinguished. These medals, rooted in history and tradition, recognize persons of heroic achievement and unselfish devotion in service to their country. Through this venerable tradition, Congress has expressed public gratitude on behalf of the nation for distinguished contributions for more than two centuries. The first medal was authorized for George Washington on March 25, 1776, and has been followed by such notable figures as Sir Winston Churchill, General Douglas MacArthur, and General Colin Powell. As the Navajo code talkers approach the final chapter of their lives, it seemed only fitting that the nation honors them by adding their names to these prestigious ranks.

The bill, "Honoring the Navajo Code Talkers," was introduced on the Senate floor on April 12, 2001, and slowly gained bi-partisan support. At first, the bill met with some legislative obstacles, but honoring the Navajo code talkers transcended politics. Senator Ben Nighthorse Campbell pointed out that just 77 years before World War II, the grandfathers of these heroes were forced from their homeland with other Navajos and interned at Bosque Redondo for four years. For these men and their comrades to rise above that injustice in American history and put their lives on the line speaks of their character and their patriotism. But just as important, it speaks to the character of our nation—we as Americans, individually and as a whole, will rise above adversity and divisiveness to unify and fight for the greater good. With the help of Senators Ben Nighthorse Campbell, Ted Stevens, and Daniel Inouye (a veteran and Congressional Medal of Honor recipient), the bill reached final passage and was signed into law by the President on December 21, 2000.

As a nation, we are the beneficiary of the accomplishments, the contributions, and the sacrifice in the struggle for freedom and democracy of those who come before us. As we face our current struggles and uncertain times ahead, it is certainly good to know we have such notable and excellent examples to follow. Perhaps John Brown, Jr., speaking for the Navajo code talkers at the Congressional Gold Medal ceremony in the Capitol Rotunda, summarized it best:

> "Of the original 29 Code Talkers, there are just five of us that live today—Chester Nez, Lloyd Oliver, Alan Dale June, Joe Palmer, and myself. We have seen much in our lives—we have experienced war and peace, we know the value of freedom and democracy that this great nation embodies. But, our experiences have also shown us how fragile these things can be, and how we must stay ever vigilant to protect them. As Code Talkers—as Marines—we did our part to protect these values. It is my hope that our young people will carry on this honorable tradition as long as the grass shall grow and the rivers flow."

To these Native American veterans I say, please accept our heartfelt and sincere congratulations as we finally mark that place in history so long overdue the Navajo code talkers.

OPPOSITE: Private Leslie Helmstreet, a Navajo Marine from Crystal, New Mexico, beating a native drum during his tour of duty in Japan in 1945.

"A Story that Needs to be Told"

RUMBLINGS of a film about the Navajo code talkers of World War II had been circulating in Hollywood for decades, but not until 1999 did the story connect with the producers and screenwriters who could weave the facts into a drama suitable for a feature film.

The idea for *Windtalkers* was first hatched ten years ago when producer Alison Rosenzweig heard about the Navajo code talkers from her brother Seth, a World War II aficionado. He had long been fascinated by their heroic contribution to the war in the Pacific and encouraged her to develop a movie about this relatively unknown chapter in American and Marine history. "I was absolutely compelled, but felt their story would make a great documentary and not necessarily material for a feature film," she said.

The idea fell to the wayside for the eight years while Rosenzweig pursued other projects. In 1999, she shared her knowledge of the Navajo code talkers with producing partner Tracie Graham. Although enthralled, Graham was equally perplexed as to how to translate the factual account into a movie narrative. Determined to uncover a dramatic element upon which to revolve the story, Rosenzweig delved into history books and eventually stumbled upon the Marine bodyguard connection. "Some code talkers were assigned Marine bodyguards for protection, but the code itself was to be considered more important than the code talker," she said. "The bodyguards' overt mission was to protect them, but their covert mission was to make sure they didn't fall into the hands of the Japanese." With the bodyguard connection and all its moral implications, the producers realized they had their story.

Rosenzweig and Graham presented their idea to screenwriters John Rice (Graham's husband) and Joe Batteer. They believed that this story was the perfect vehicle to reunite the two writers, former partners who years earlier had amicably parted to pursue solo careers. "Happily," Rosenzweig said, "they both loved the idea."

"Tracie and Alison essentially gave us a one-liner that we thought was terrific," said Rice. "A man is given complex and morally challenging orders and has to make a decision, a decision that could only be presented in the heightened circumstances of war." Batteer added, "The story of the Navajo and their contribution to the Marine Corps in World War II is amazing. But in particular,

we were struck by the idea that Navajo code talkers had bodyguards who, in some forward units, were really there to protect the code and apparently had been given orders to take out the code talker should he fall into enemy hands."

Fortunately, this outcome never came to pass in World War II. But the notion that a Marine might have had to kill one of his own, presumably someone with whom he had developed a bond, resonated with the writers. This moral dilemma—played out in the character of Corporal Joe Enders portrayed by Nicolas Cage—became the foundation for the story.

Screenwriters Rice and Batteer read everything they could find about the Marines and the code talkers in the Pacific theater of the

ABOVE: Among the first assault waves to hit the beaches of Saipan in June 1944 (from left to right). Corporal Oscar B. Iithma of Gallup, New Mexico; PFC Jack Nez of Fort Defiance, Arizona; and PFC Carl C. Gorman of Chinle, Arizona.

> *"I think the audience, aside from being entertained, will learn a lot about the code talkers' contribution to the victory of the Second World War and will be inspired by the film's celebration of the human spirit."*
> —PRODUCER TERENCE CHANG

war. They decided to set their story against the backdrop of the Battle of Saipan, and developed scenes that directly evolved from anecdotal accounts they read. For example, Batteer says, "There were instances when Navajo were mistaken for Japanese by U.S. Marines. Protecting them from their own men, ironically, was another reason why some Navajo were assigned bodyguards."

Rice credits the title, *Windtalkers*, to the Navajo culture. "Wind figures prominently in the Navajo scheme of things, culturally and religiously, and it just feels very ethereal. We wanted to imbue the piece with a sense of this Navajo spirituality."

Without a written script, but on the strength of a thoroughly developed narrative outline, director John Woo and his longtime production partner Terence Chang agreed to meet with the two writers and producers Rosenzweig and Graham. "There was no script, just a verbal pitch," recalled Chang. "But Joe and John are very good storytellers." At the end of the writers' lengthy delivery of their

ABOVE: PFC Gorman of Chinle, Arizona, manning an observation post in June 1944, as Marines consolidate their position on Saipan.

24

story, Woo stood up and clapped, saying, "That's my kind of movie!"

"It was a great day," said Rosenzweig, "because John Woo had always been our fantasy director for this movie."

"I fell in love with the story the minute I heard it," Chang said. "It's so emotional. It's a celebration of the human spirit. And it is a story that needs to be told."

The development and pre-production process moved smoothly from that point. "You can develop projects for years," said Chang, "but *Windtalkers* had been so thoroughly worked out that the first actual draft of the script was almost identical to what we had heard in the pitch and been captured by." With a solid screenplay and Woo on board, Chang had no trouble enlisting financial backing from MGM. At the time, Woo had just completed filming *Face/Off* and had enjoyed a very cohesive working relationship with Oscar®-winning actor Nicolas Cage. He immediately thought of him for *Windtalkers'* lead role, and Cage became the first actor to sign on to the project.

Seeing the Navajo code talkers' story brought to life in a major

motion picture at last, producer Rosenzweig achieved a dream that had been many years in the making. The code talkers—little-known American heroes—would finally be given the widespread commemoration they deserved. "They were not only incredibly brave soldiers," said Rosenzweig, "but they were also brilliant. They created this code based on their language, memorized it, and never made mistakes. I just cannot believe that with bombs going off all around them and bullets whizzing by, these men calmly and courageously were able to perform their duty flawlessly. It's an embarrassment to me that the world does not yet know about these brave heroes who risked their lives for their country. They are unsung heroes. Bringing this knowledge to the world, I couldn't be any prouder."

ABOVE: Marines PFC George H. Kirk of Ganado, Arizona, and PFC John V. Goodluck of Lukachukai, Arizona, in Guam. OPPOSITE: Navajo Indians Corp. Henry Bake, Jr., (left) and PFC George H. Kirk operate a portable radio set behind the front lines in December 1943.

The Code Talkers

MORE than 3,600 young Navajo men and women joined the armed forces during World War II. Among them were approximately 400 men who served in the Marines as code talkers, providing 100-percent secure battlefield communications through a complex code based on their native language. The Japanese never unlocked the code, and the Navajo code talkers were later acknowledged as significant contributors to U.S. victories in the Pacific.

Communication security is crucial on the battlefield, but until the development of the Navajo code the military had never devised a perfect, foolproof system. The strength of the Navajo code lay in the language's rarity and complexity. The Navajo language, at the time, was purely vocal; it had no written form, alphabet, or symbols. It was only spoken by those who lived in the Navajo Nation in the Southwest United States and by a handful of non-Indians, primarily anthropologists. The code that developed out of this ancient, unwritten language was unbreakable, and it became the Marines' greatest secret weapon in the Pacific.

The Navajo code talker program was the brainchild of Philip Johnston, a missionary's son raised on Navajo lands and one of the few non-Indians in the world who spoke fluent Navajo. A World War I veteran, civil engineer, photographer, journalist, and author, Johnston frequently gave lectures about Navajo culture and his childhood years living with the Diné, "the people," as the Navajo call themselves. At the age of nine he accompanied his father and two Navajo leaders to Washington, D.C., to act as the translator in a meeting with President Theodore Roosevelt about fair treatment of the Navajo and Hopi.

When America entered the war after the Japanese invasion of Pearl Harbor, Johnston learned that the military resumed its work on Indian-language-based codes that had been attempted during World War I. There were serious problems with these codes, however, because the Indian languages had no equivalents for military terms.

Johnston was certain that security would be guaranteed with a Navajo-based military code. In February 1942, he took his idea to

OPPOSITE: PFC Preston Toledo (left) and his cousin PFC Frank Toledo, Navajo, attached to a Marine Artillery Regiment in the South Pacific, in July 1943.

SETTING UP SHOP

We used several types of radio sets. The TBX unit was the one that we used most. It weighed about 80 pounds—very heavy to lug around. We had two sets: a transmitter and a receiver, connected with junky cable. We tried to set the generator on a bench of some kind when we could, so we could straddle the bench and crank the thing. But this didn't work on a location where it was sandy. So the coconut tree came in very handy. We hooked the generator to the trunk, straddled the tree and cranked. It took two men—one to crank the generator and get the juice going into the mike, and the other to transmit the message. We got information off the ship [the transport] after a landing, and kept those in charge of the operation informed.

One thing we learned in school was not to be on the air longer than was absolutely necessary. We had to be careful not to repeat words in a sentence—that is, if the message had to go through more than once, we tried to say it differently every time.

—A code talker on Guadalcanal as quoted in The Navajo Code Talkers, *by Doris A. Paul*

Major General Clayton B. Vogel and other officers at Camp Elliott in California. With the help of four Navajos from Los Angeles and one from San Diego, Johnston set up a demonstration involving a simulated battlefield situation. He asked a Marine officer to write out typical combat messages and hand it to a Navajo who would translate it into his own language. The Navajo then used a field radio to voice the message to another Navajo. The second Navajo translated the message into English and passed it onto another Marine officer. The test was a complete success—the messages were relayed quickly and accurately. General Vogel recommended that 200 Navajos be recruited into the Marine Corps to be utilized as code talkers. His recommendation was approved, but on a smaller scale—the first recruitment was limited to only 30 men.

With the permission of the Navajo Tribal Council, recruiting began at Window Rock, Arizona, in May 1942. The Marines enlisted 29 young men in good physical condition, fluent in both Navajo and English, to make up the first platoon of code talkers.

PRAYERS ON THE BATTLEFIELD

I was 18 when I entered the service, on very short notice. . . . I was working at the hospital in Fort Defiance when I suddenly made up my mind to join the Marines.

I did pray many, many times when I was exposed to danger on the main battleline, as a code talker and as a signalman. I prayed as my mother and father had taught me—to the Heavenly Being as well as to Mother Earth.

Now when I came back, surprisingly my mother told me, "Son, do you know that since you left, almost every morning, I have gone to my sacred hill and prayed, using my sacred corn pollen, that you would come back with your whole physical being and a good mind." Maybe that is the reason I came back all in one piece. . . . I think my mother's prayers on her sacred hill helped me through the war and after I got back home.

—*A code talker as quoted in* The Navajo Code Talkers, *by Doris A. Paul*

THIS PAGE: *Code talkers in formation at Camp Elliott, California, ca. 1942.*

"The Navajo code talkers are sacred and precious jewels, and should be respected and treated as such. They are our own heroes."

—ACTOR ROGER WILLIE

Further testing under battle conditions in the Pacific proved that the Navajo code was superior in every way. Classified messages could be translated into Navajo, transmitted via radio or walkie-talkie, received and translated back into English in 20 seconds. The same process done by an encoding machine took 30 minutes. Johnston was made a staff sergeant and given the job of supervising the Navajo Marines in training for the top-secret code talker program at Camp Pendleton in Oceanside, California. Recruiting orders eventually expanded, and by the end of the war, an estimated 400 Navajo were enlisted as code talkers.

New recruits began their service in boot camp at the San Diego Marine Corps Recruit Depot. From there they began their code talker training at the Field Signal Battalion Training Center at Camp Pendleton. The first 29 code talkers created the actual code, assigning Navajo words to hundreds of military terms. Marine Corps units, for example, were given Navajo clan names and airplanes given the names of birds. "Besh-lo," the Navajo word for iron-fish, meant "submarine"; "dah-he-tih," or hummingbird, meant "fighter plane"; and "debeh-li-zine," or black street, stood for "squad." Because the repetition of letters is a common clue used by cryptologists to crack a code, each of the six most commonly used letters of the alphabet were assigned three code names. The second six most repeated letters were given two code names. This allowed code talkers to send the same word in a variety of different ways and made the code very complex.

After the code was created by the first class of 29, the training course was organized. The program was divided into three sections, the first of which was devoted to memorization. Bringing code-talker dictionaries into the field was out of the question, as they could fall into enemy hands. Therefore, each code talker had to memorize the code alphabet and 211-word vocabulary list.

The second stage of training involved putting the code to use by translating orders from the Marine Corps training manual. Code talkers were drilled with orders read aloud by two Navajo from the original group, John Benally and Johnny Manuelito, who had stayed behind to teach. Students translated the spoken commands into English and neatly printed the translated message on paper. Throughout their training, the class was graded on penmanship as well as accuracy because messages given in the field—often written under great stress as gunfire and bombing raged around the code talker—had to be clearly legible.

In the third stage, the code talkers learned how to set up and operate radios, field telephones, and other communications equipment. They practiced drills in field exercises, and at the end of this two-week stage were ready to be shipped out.

In addition to language skills, code-talker recruits were scrutinized for physical ability, intelligence, and character during their eight weeks at Camp Pendleton. Each trainee had to meet the exacting standards set by Jimmie King, a Navajo who became a teacher in the program. King assumed the responsibility of graduating only perfectly qualified code talkers. He considered a man's character as important as his language ability because of the threat of capture and torture that faced everyone in combat. Code talkers were expected to have the strength of character to submit to torture and

---

NO ERRORS

The entire operation [Iwo Jima] was directed by Navajo code. Our corps command post was on a battleship from which orders went to the three division command posts on the beachhead, and on down to the lower echelons. I was signal officer of the Fifth Division. During the first 48 hours, while we were landing and consolidating our shore positions, I had six Navajo radio nests operating around the clock. In that period alone they sent and received over 800 messages without an error.

Weeks later, when our flag was raised over Mount Suribachi, word of that event came in the Navajo code.

—*Major Howard M. Conner as quoted in*
The Navajo Code Talkers, *by Doris A. Paul*

OPPOSITE: *Pvt. Jimmy D. Benallie of Gallup, New Mexico, in front of the Arakaki Bicycle Shop in Okinawa in April 1945.*

アラカキ自轉車店

**THE FIRST 29 NAVAJO
CODE TALKERS**

382nd Platoon, United States Marines

Charlie Begay

Roy L. Begay

Samuel H. Begay

John Ashi Benally

Wilsie Bitsie

Cosey S. Brown

John Brown, Jr.

John Chee

Benjamin Cleveland

Eugene R. Crawford

David Curley

Lowell S. Damon

George H. Dennison

James Dixon

Carl N. Gorman

Oscar B. Ilthma

Allen Dale June

Alfred Leonard

Johnny R. Manuelito

William McCabe

Chester Nez

Jack Nez

Lloyd Oliver

Joe Palmer

Frank Danny Pete

Nelson S. Thompson

Harry Tsosie

John Willie, Jr.

William Yazzie

THE ENEMY WAY: NAVAJO HEALING CEREMONY

The Enemy Way is a three-day ceremony in which the diagnostician, the herb man, and the medicine man take part. The diagnostician will tell the man what his trouble is, the herb man will prescribe herbs, and the medicine man will perform the ceremony of purification.

The medicine man has a bundle in which he places anything related to the enemy—a coat, eyeglasses, weapon—anything the Navajo may have brought back from the combat area. Some had been known to bring back skulls or parts of the enemy's bones.

The code talkers returned with bayonets, helmets, tufts of hair from Japanese victims, bits of clothing, objects taken from pockets of the enemy's uniforms, etc.

Sometimes a hole is dug, the souvenirs buried and shot at with a rifle four times, thus cutting off all bad communications between the mind of the Navajo and the enemy—feelings of guilt or regret that are causing the sickness. . . . There is a unifying influence present with everyone involved contributing to the healing of the returnee. He is thus brought back into harmony with nature. . . . The rites help to disentangle a man from his past.

—*From* The Navajo Code Talkers, *by Doris A. Paul*

"What these men did is incredible. I'm honored to have been involved in the film and to help bring their accomplishments to the public eye."

—ACTOR NICOLAS CAGE

mistaken for Japanese by their fellow soldiers, and in a few instances, they were captured by Marines and had to explain that they were on the same side.

The code talkers—praised for their speed, skill, and accuracy—were vital to American victories at Guadalcanal, Tarawa, Peleliu, Iwo Jima, and other Pacific battle zones. "Were it not for the Navajos," declared Major Howard Connor, 5th Marine Division signal officer, "the Marines would never have taken Iwo Jima." The Japanese never deciphered the code, which was laced with a spectrum of high and low inflections similar to a Chinese dialect, and the secret weapon was a resounding success.

The Navajo fulfilled their missions as outstanding code talkers as well as exemplary Marines. The Navajo code was not declassified until 1968, and more than three decades later the U.S. Congress acknowledged the code talkers' service to their country by awarding them Congressional Gold Medals. Most of the medals were awarded posthumously, but there were four code talkers present at the Congressional Medal award ceremony in Washington, D.C., in July 2001, in which President George W. Bush personally presented the medals.

never give up the top-secret weapon that existed only in their minds. Jimmie King would only accept enlistees into the program who met all these criteria and who could be trusted implicitly in battle. "You could trust that man," he said of a code talker graduate. "He would lay his life down, just like we would, before we would tell what this (the code) was." David E. Patterson, a code talker who served in the 4th Marine Division, said, "When I was inducted into the service, one of the commitments I made was that I was willing to die for my country— the U.S., the Navajo Nation, and my family. My [native] language was my weapon."

The Navajo code talkers took part in every Marine assault in the Pacific, from Guadalcanal in 1942 to Okinawa in 1945. They served in all six divisions of the Marines, including the parachute units, and much of their work was done during actual combat. Navajo Marines were sometimes

OPPOSITE: Marine PFC Cecil G. Trosip of Oraibi, Arizona, at his communication system on Saipan in July 1945. ABOVE: Hasbro's CodeTalker G.I. Joe Action Figure, produced in 2001. ABOVE CENTER: The Iwo Jima Commemorative Stamp, issued in 1945, shows Ira Hayes, a Pima Indian and U.S. Marine (first on left) stretching to help raise the U.S. flag.

35

Paul Edward Tso, Sr.
6th Marine Division

"I was afraid of nothing. I felt if I was going to end my life in war, that was the way it was to be."

Warrior Legends

DURING a visit to Window Rock, Arizona, in 1975, Japanese photographer Kenji Kawano met many Navajo, including Carl N. Gorman, one of the original 29 code talkers. He developed great admiration for the code talkers and was eventually made the official photographer for the Navajo Code Talkers Association—as well as an honorary member. In 1990, he published an eloquent collection of photographs and interviews entitled *Warriors: Navajo Code Talkers*, excerpted here and on the following two pages.

Thomas H. Begay
5th Marine Division (*Below*)

"We were disciplined . . . I learned to survive combat. The first hour, I was with my radio, communicating with other floats. I was scared, very scared, mortars and artillery were landing everywhere, but I wasn't hit. The Iwo Jima sand was ashy and hard to walk on, but I had to carry my radio and other equipment across it. I was sent to replace Pfc. Paul Kinlacheeny, who was killed on the beach.

"I was awarded six battle stars during my military career for being in major battles from Iwo Jima to the Korean War. I was never wounded or shot but was missed by inches, and missed being captured by thirty minutes or less. I was very lucky to have gotten through that time. Maybe because I believe in the traditional Navajo ways and felt that the Great Spirit was protecting me. My parents, both very traditional Navajos, had ceremonies for me using clothes that I had worn before I left home to go in the service. These ceremonies protected my well-being, so I could survive."

Samuel Tom Holiday
4th Marine Division (*Above*)

"A week after landing on the shores of Saipan during World War II, a fellow Navajo code talker and I were in a prone position, discussing the fact that we didn't have a chance if we moved. I put my helmet [on my rifle] and raised it out of the foxhole, and shots sprayed across our position.

"We stayed down, waiting. The shouts and screams of fellow soldiers were all around us, and we thought these were our last minutes on earth. Suddenly, I heard a deep 'THUMP' next to me, where my fellow code talker was lying, and I was scared I would be next. It took every ounce of courage I had to look over at him—I expected blood and guts. To my relief—and the relief of my foxhole partner—I saw one of the biggest bullfrogs I'd ever seen on my partner's back."

Francis T. Thompson
2nd, 8th Marine Divisions

"I lost my dad while I was overseas, and that hurt the most. Facing the enemy at Saipan and seeing my buddies killed all around me was very bad."

George H. Kirk, Sr.
3rd Marine Division

"The Japanese were preparing to attack an American installation on Guam. Our Marine reconnaissance found their location and the code talkers sent a message to a battleship and two artillery units to tell them where the target was. The Japanese were wiped out and our commander, Major General Erikine, was saved by our language."

Raphael D. Yazzie
4th Marine Division (*Above*)

"At one point on the front line in Iwo Jima, during a barrage of guns and rockets, we received orders by radio to assist in the rescue of our platoon, which was under fire. We did, and got all of our men safely back to our regiment."

John Pinto
New Mexico State Senator

"I liked the Marines . . . they gave me basic training, good food, and a scholarship. After I was discharged, I was able to go to school."

David Jordan
3rd Marine Division (*Below*)

"It was two or three days after we hit the island in Bougainville that our sergeant told me to go to the rear where the command post was. I got lost, and it began to get dark. An Army security guard shoved his gun in my back and took my rifle away because he thought I was Japanese. I told him who I was and that I was looking for the message center. He took me to camp headquarters, where another Navajo soldier recognized me. I was freed after that."

Pahe D. Yazzie
5th Marine Division

"I volunteered to serve my country."

Eugene Crawford
1st Marine Division

"At one point I was captured by U.S. Army soldiers, who thought I was Japanese."

Albert Smith
4th, 14th, 23rd Marine Divisions

"I walked the full length of Saipan and Tinian islands carrying maps and escorting replacements, prisoners, and farmers. At the same time, I operated the radio for the riflemen and was under fire myself while delivering messages."

The Battle of Saipan

THE battle scenes in *Windtalkers* recreate the United State's fight for Saipan, a pivotal battle considered the beginning of the end of the war in the Pacific. A mammoth invasion fleet—Operation Forager—struck at the island which had been under Japanese control since World War I. High on Mount Topachau at the center of Saipan lie bunkers in which Japanese Army commander General Saito and Navy commander Admiral Nagumo directed their defense strategies.

In the following essay, Lyn Kukral of the U.S. Marine Corps Historical Center provides the basic facts of this decisive battle:

D-Day for Saipan, headquarters of Japan's Central Pacific Fleet, was June 15, 1944. The island's Japanese defenders numbered almost 30,000. While the Navy landed 8,000 Marines from the 2nd and 4th Divisions in the first 20 minutes of the assault, Japanese shoreline defenses kept the invasion force fighting for three days to protect the beachhead.

Naval bombardment on the first day was insufficient, although it improved to the point that one Japanese officer credited it as the single greatest factor in the American victory. Four battleships, five cruisers, and 39 destroyers provided on-call fire, with destroyers taking out enemy gun positions and the larger ships assigned to saturation bombardment. Gunboats, converted infantry landing craft, were especially effective against the caves because their shallow draft allowed them to move in close to shore. Illumination from Navy-launched star shells helped the Marines protect their lines at night.

Saipan's mountainous terrain made seizure of the approximately 14-mile-long by 6-mile-wide island an arduous process for the Marines and the 27th Infantry Division. Prolonged hand-to-hand combat characterized the campaign. In addition to the fierce enemy resistance and the logistical problems caused by the sheer size of the U.S. force, the mix of unfamiliar Army and Marine units made coordinating their movements difficult.

From their original beachheads on the island's southwest coast, it took the 4th Division Marines until July 9 to reach Marpi Point at Saipan's northern tip. There, the remaining defenders and a number of Japanese civilians jumped from the high cliffs rather than surrender; estimates of the total number of civilians who killed themselves on Saipan run as high as 22,000. All but a thousand of the Japanese defenders died in battle or by their own hands. U.S. casualties on Saipan were 16,612; 13,000 were Marines. Due to the difficulties on Saipan, the invasion of Guam, scheduled for June 18, was postponed until late July.

RIGHT: Marines on Saipan using an ox cart to transport supplies to the front lines, June 1944. FOLLOWING PAGE: The first wave of Marines to hit the Saipan beach take cover behind a sand dune, June 1944.

A DEAFENING BLAST

About sundown [off Saipan] I was told to make a call to shore. The first wave had hit the shore when I radioed, "How is it on the island?" The answer was "Pretty rough. They're being killed all around." That evening when I went in, our boat turned over before we landed, about 300 yards from the beach. I was almost drowned. I took off my pack, but somehow it got caught on something—maybe it was my gas mask that I hadn't taken off. So I was dragging that pack. As I was coming ashore someone cut off the pack with a combat knife, and dragged me up on shore. Water was coming out of my mouth and nose; but I survived, and we found our company that night.

The next morning another guy and I went down to shore to get that pack. We saw a lot of Marines that had been killed, still on the beach. . . . About that time a tank landed and we followed it, which we found wasn't too bright an idea. The Japs zeroed in on that tank and started throwing mortar shells on it. A shell exploded right near me. I felt funny all over—my head felt enormous! It was like that for a week.

—A code talker as quoted in The Navajo Code Talkers, *by Doris A. Paul*

"The stage of Windtalkers *is the Battle of Saipan in 1944, a bloody and horrifying episode in the war in the Pacific. It is my hope that* Windtalkers *shows that war is, and always has been, the worst way to work out our differences."*

—DIRECTOR JOHN WOO

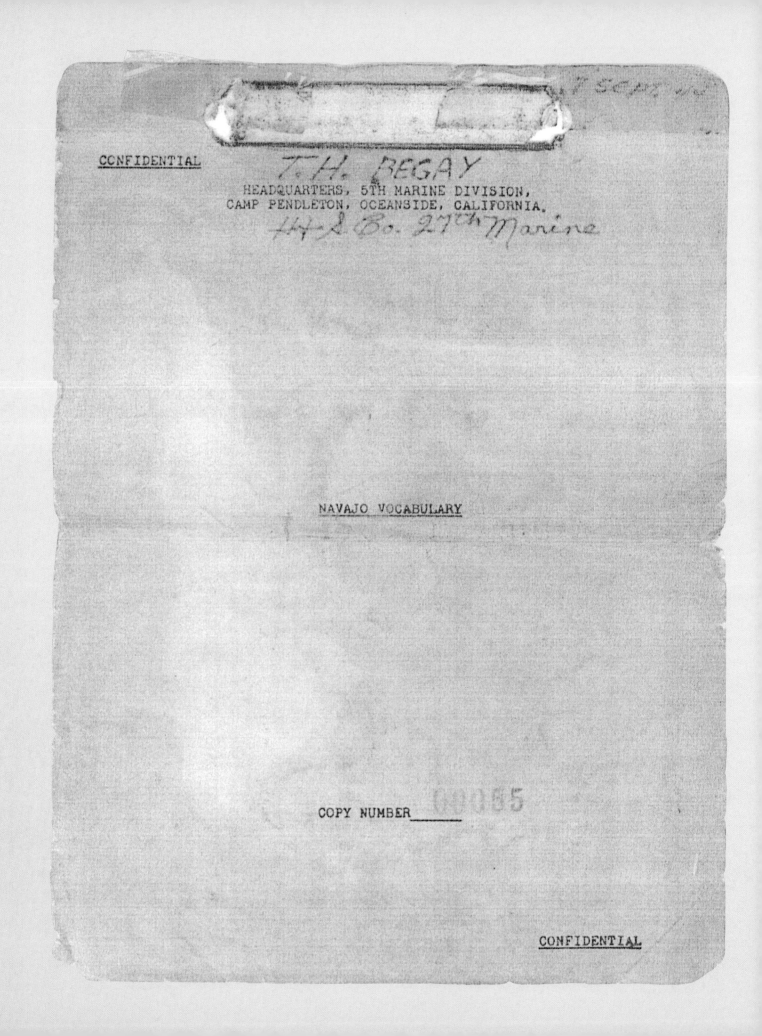

7 SEPT 44

CONFIDENTIAL

T.H. BEGAY

HEADQUARTERS, 5TH MARINE DIVISION,
CAMP PENDLETON, OCEANSIDE, CALIFORNIA.

Hq & Co. 27th Marine

NAVAJO VOCABULARY

COPY NUMBER ___ 00065

The Navajo Code Talker Dictionary (Excerpts)

WORD	NAVAJO WORD	LITERAL TRANSLATION	WORD	NAVAJO WORD	LITERAL TRANSLATION
NAMES OF VARIOUS ORGANIZATIONS			Bivouac	Ehl-nas-teh	Brush shelter
Corps	Din-neh-ih	Clan	Bomb	A-ye-shi	Eggs
Division	Ashih-hi	Salt	Booby trap	Dineh-ba-whoa-blehi	Man trap
Regiment	Tabaha	Edge water			
Battalion	Tacheene	Red soil	Camp	To-altseh-hogan	Temporary place
Company	Nakia	Mexican	Camouflage	Di-nes-ih	Hid
Platoon	Has-clish-nih	Mud	Casualty	Bih-din-ne-dey	Put out of action
Section	Yo-ih	Beads			
Squad	Debeh-li-zini	Black sheep	Ceiling	Da-tel-jay	Seal
			Cemetary	Jish-cha	Among devils
NAMES OF AIRPLANES					
Planes	Wo-tah-de-ne-ih	Air force	Detail	Vbe-beh-sha	Deer tail
Dive bomber	Gini	Chicken hawk	Detonator	Ah-deel-tahi (or)	Blown up
Torpedo plane	Tas-chizzie	Swallow	Disembark	Eh-ha-jay	Get out
Obs. plan	Ne-as-jah	Owl			
Fighter plane	Da-he-tih-hi	Humming bird	Encounter	Bi-khanh	Go against
Bomber plane	Jay-sho	Buzzard	Engage	A-ha-ne-ho-ta	Agreed
Patrol plane	Ga-gih	Crow	Enlarge	Nih-tsa-goh-al-neh	Make big
Transport	Atsah	Eagle			
			Farm	Mai-be-he-ahgan	Fox arm
NAMES OF SHIPS			Fierce	Toh-bah-ha-zsid	Afraid
Ships	Toh-dineh-ih	Sea force	File	Ba-eh-chez	File
Battleship	Lo-tso	Whale	Flare	Wo-chi	Light streak
Aircraft	Tsidi-moffa-ye-hi	Bird carrier	Flight	Ma-e-as-zloli	Fox light
Submarine	Besh-lo	Iron fish	Force	Ta-na-ne-ladi	Without care
Mine sweeper	Cha	Beaver	Fortification	Ah-na-sozi	Cliff dwelling
Destroyer	Ca-lo	Shark	Forward	Tehi	Let's go
Transport	Dineh-nay-ye-hi	Man carrier			
Cruiser	Lo-tso-yazzie	Small whale	Hospital	A-zey-al-ih	Place of medicine
Mosquito boat	Tse-e	Mosquito	Hostile	A-nah-ne-dzin	Not friendly
			Howitzer	Be-el-don-ts-quodi	Short big gun
VOCABULARY					
Abandon	Ye-tsan	Run away from	Machine gun	A-knah-as-donih	Rapid fire gun
Accomplish	Ul-so	All done	Magnetic	Na-e-lahi	Pick up
According	Be-ka-ho	According to	Minute	Ah-khay-el-kit-yazzie	Little hour
Action	Ah-ha-tinh	Place of action	Mortar	Be-al-doh-cid-da-hi	Sitting gun
Been	Tses-nah-nes-chee	Bee nut	Motor	Chide-be-tse-tsen	Car head
Begin	Ha-hol-ziz	Commence from			
Belong	Tses-nah-snez	Long bee	Navy	Tal-kah-silago	Sea soldier
			Negative	Do-ya-sho-da	No good
			Not	Ni-dah-than-zie	No turkey
			Notice	Ne-da-tazi-thin	No turkey ice

OPPOSITE: The cover page from Thomas Begay's copy of the Navajo Code Talker Manual.

WORD	NAVAJO WORD	LITERAL TRANSLATION	WORD	NAVAJO WORD	LITERAL TRANSLATION
Pill box	Bi-so-dih-dot-sahi-bi-tsah	Sick pig box	Tank	Chay-da-gahi	Tortoise
Plane	Tsidi	Bird	Torpedo	Lo-be-ca	Fish shell
Pontoon	tkosh-jah-da-na-elt	Floating barrel	Village	Chah-ho-oh-lhan-ih	Many shelter
Pyrotechnic	coh-na-chanh	Fancy fire	When	Gloe-eh-na-ah-wo-hai	Weasel hen
Reef	Tsa-zhin	Black rock	Where	Gloe-ih-qui-ah	Weasel here
Report	Tho-neh	Got word	Which	Gloe-ih-a-hsi-tlon	Weasel tied together
River	Toh-yil-kal	Much water			
Robot bomb	A-ye-shi-na-tah-ih	Egg fly			
Rocket	Lesz-yil-beshi	Sand boil			
Route	Gah-bih-tkeen	Rabbit trail			

(For the complete Navajo Code Talkers Dictionary, see page 116.)

Saboteur	A-tkel-el-ini	Trouble maker
Sailor	Cha-le-gai	White caps
Sniper	Oh-behi	Pick 'em off
Stream	Toh-ni-lih	Running water
Success	Ut-zah	It is done

BELOW: Navajo Marine fighters serving with a Signal Unit. (Front row, left to right) Privates Earl Johnny, Kee Etsicitty, and John V. Goodluck, and PFC David Jordan, (back row, left to right) Privates Jack C. Morgan, George H. Kirk, and Tom H. Jones, and Corporal Henry Bake, Jr. OPPOSITE: Page two of Thomas Begay's Navajo Code Talker Manual.

CONFIDENTIAL

NAMES OF ORGANIZATIONS (Con't)

MILITARY MEANING	NAVAJO PRONUNCIATION	NAVAJO MEANING
Battalion	Tacheene	Red Soil
Company	Nakia	Mexican
Platoon	Has-clish-nih	Mud
Section	Yo-ih	Beads
Squad	Debeh-li-zini	Black Sheep

COMMUNICATION NAMES

MILITARY MEANING	NAVAJO PRONUNCIATION	NAVAJO MEANING
Telephone	Besh-hal-ne-ih	Telephone
Switchboard	Ya-ih-e-tih-ih	Central
Wire	Besh-le-chee-ih	Copper
Telegraph	Besh-le-chee-ih-beh-hane-ih	Comm by copper wire
Semaphore	Dah-na-a-tah-ih-beh-hane-ih	Flag Signals
Blinker	Coh-nil-kol-lih	Fire Blinder
Radio	Nil-chi-hal-ne-ih	Radio
Panels	Az-kad-be-ha-ne-ih	Carpet Signals

OFFICERS NAMES

MILITARY MEANING	NAVAJO PRONUNCIATION	NAVAJO MEANING
Officers	A-la-jih-na-zini	Headmen
Major General	So-na-kih	Two stars
Brigadier General	So-a-la-ih	One star
Colonel	Atsah-besh-le-gai	Silver Eagle
Lt.Colonel	Che-chil-be-tah-besh-legai	Silver Oak Leaf
Major	Che-chil-be-tah-ola	Gold Oak Leaf
Captain	Besh-legai-na-kih	Two Silver Bars
1st Lieutenant	Besh-legai-a-lah-ih	One Silver Bar
2d Lieutenant	Ola-alah-ih-ni-ahi	One Gold Bar

AIRPLANE NAMES

MILITARY MEANING	NAVAJO PRONUNCIATION	NAVAJO MEANING
Airplanes	Wo-tah-de-ne-ih	Air Force
Dive Bomber	Gini	Chicken Hawk
Torpedo Plane	Tas-chizzie	Swallow
Observation Plane	Ne-as-jah	Owl
Fighter Plane	Da-he-tih-hi	Humming Bird
Bomber	Jay-sho	Buzzard
Patrol Plane	Ga-gih	Crow
Transport Plane	Atsah	Eagle

SHIPS NAMES

MILITARY MEANING	NAVAJO PRONUNCIATION	NAVAJO MEANING
Ships	Toh-dineh-ih	Sea Force
Battleship	Lo-tso	Whale
Aircraft Carrier	Tsidi-ney-ye-hi	Bird Carrier
Submarine	Besh-lo	Iron Fish

CONFIDENTIAL

-2-

Navajo Nation

"MANY people have asked us why we fight the white man's wars," said Raymond Nakai, Chairman of the Navajo Tribal Council, in 1969. "Our answer is always that we are proud to be American, and we are proud to be American Indians. . . . The American Indian always stands ready when his country needs him." The Navajo people have a long history of defending their lands in battle, and to code talker and *Windtalkers* consultant Albert Smith, World War II "was about land, and we fought for our people, our land and our country."

The Native Americans who would become known as the Navajo migrated from the northern areas of the continent and set-

tled in the American Southwest in the 1500s. One group continued further southward into what is now Arizona, and became the Apache Tribe. The widely scattered Navajo people were not ruled by one chief but divided into independently ruled family clans separated by miles of grazing land. Each clan community was a cluster of hogans—round, wood houses covered in mud and clay—surrounded by cornfields and grazing lands for goats, horses, and sheep.

The headman of each clan had the authority to make treaties with other clans, but the vastness of Navajo territory made it impossible for everyone to know about every treaty. Clans raided other clans over disputed grazing lands, and through many generations, the Navajo also battled to defend their territory against Spanish settlers; neighboring Hopi, Pueblo, and Zuni Tribes; and white settlers.

At the end of the Mexican War in 1848, the United States won half of Mexico's territory, including the region that made up the

OPPOSITE: A small ruin at Black Mesa, near the Painted Desert in northern Arizona in 1932. ABOVE: Map of the Navajo Nation, 2001.

"I visited the Navajo Nation twice to meet with some the surviving code talkers. I expressed our sincere interest in telling their story with this film, and asked them to give us their blessing. We were very concerned about making the film as culturally and historically accurate as possible."

—Producer Terence Chang

Navajo homeland. The following year, the U.S. government made a treaty with Navajo leader Mariano Martinez that gave the United States jurisdiction over the entire Navajo Tribe. Even though Martinez only represented one group of Navajo, the treaty stated that the agreement applied to every clan throughout the territory. With white people swiftly encroaching on Navajo lands in a Southwest gold rush, skirmishes broke out between Navajo clans and U.S. soldiers ordered to protect the settlers.

Full-fledged war broke out in 1860 when more than 1,000 Navajo attacked Fort Defiance. They were driven back by the U.S. Army's superior firepower, but the raid ignited the Navajo Wars— the nation's new policy to wage all-out war with the Navajo who posed a significant threat to the Army and to western expansion.

Indian agent and soldier Kit Carson used a "scorch and burn" policy to strip the Navajo of their livelihood. He and his Army rode across the land burning crops, killing livestock, poisoning wells, and destroying hogans. The Navajo fled in all directions, but thousands gathered in the massive Canyon de Chelly in the hope of evading Carson and waiting out the war. But in the winter of 1863 Carson set up a blockage at the sole entrance to the canyon, shooting anyone who tried to leave. The trapped Navajo faced starvation for months, and in March of 1864 were forced to surrender. Carson led the 8,000 survivors on a 350-mile march to Bosque Rodondo, a reservation in New Mexico. In the "Long March," one of the saddest episodes in

American history, hundreds of men, women, and children froze to death and starved. The poor conditions at the reservation, where Apaches were also being held, led to many more deaths.

The Navajo were held at Bosque Rodondo for four years until the Peace Treaty of June 1, 1868, which granted them their own sovereign land. Two weeks after the treaty was signed, a column 10 miles long started the long walk home to the newly created Navajo reservation, a stretch of land along the New Mexico-Arizona border measuring about one-tenth the size of the lands formerly claimed by the Navajo. Although it started small, the reservation expanded steadily over the next 100 years and is now the largest reservation in the United States, covering an area more than 17 million acres.

In 1921, Congress passed the Indian Citizenship Act, granting U.S. citizenship to all Native Americans born in the United States. In the 21st century, the Navajo Nation has a population of more than 260,000. Perhaps the most powerful evidence of the Navajo's adoption of the United States, hand-in-hand with its Native American identity, is the heroic work of the Navajo code talkers of World War II, who volunteered to use their unique native language to help win the war in the Pacific.

Opposite: Antelope Ruin, Canyon de Chelly National Monument, Arizona, photographed in 1927.

52

MAJOR EVENTS IN NAVAJO HISTORY

825–1000 Athabascan people migrate from the far northwest to the southwest of what is now the United States.

1300 Athabascans break up into the separate tribes of Navajo and Apache. Navajo refer to themselves as the Diné, or "the people" (the Spanish later named them Navajo). The Diné settle within their four sacred mountains of present-day New Mexico.

1600 Spanish kidnap Navajo in New Mexico and trade them in slave labor. Active slave trade continues until the early 1900s.

1606 War breaks out between the Spanish and the Indians in New Mexico, including the Navajo.

1621 Navajo use of horses becomes widespread; begin raids against Spanish settlements and Pueblo towns.

1851 United States builds Fort Defiance, the first fort in Arizona, to control the Navajo.

1858 U.S. soldiers kill 60 head of livestock owned by Navajo headman Manuelito, who confronts the major at Fort Defiance. More soldiers burn his village and fields. Manuelito resolves to drive off the white soldiers and begins organizing Navajo headmen for war.

1860 Over 1,000 Navajo led by Manuelito attack Fort Defiance. They nearly overrun the fort, but are forced to retreat by superior gunfire; army's policy of "total war" against the Navajos begins.

1861 Fort Defiance is abandoned with the outbreak of the Civil War.

1863–1864 Kit Carson and his army volunteers drive the Navajo from their lands in a "scorch and burn" policy. Thousands go into hiding in Canyon de Chelly, and in the winter Carson sets up a blockade at the entrance. In March 1864, the troops round up the starving Navajo and send them on the Long Walk to a camp at Bosque Redondo, 350 miles away. More than 8,000 Navajo and some Apache tread through blizzards.

1868 Civil War hero General William Te-cumseh Sherman negotiates a peace treaty with the Navajo. The Treaty of Bosque Redondo is signed by 29 Navajo headmen and provides the Navajo with a reservation on the New Mexico-Arizona border that is about one-tenth of the size of their previous territory.

1882 President Chester Arthur allots 4,000 square miles of land in northern Arizona to the Hopi, igniting a Navajo-Hopi land dispute.

1922 Oil is discovered on the Navajo Reservation and the Bureau of Indian Affairs (BIA) tries to get tribal consent for leases with oil companies. The Navajo refuse to lease their land. Secretary of the Interior Albert Fall sets up bogus councils to facilitate leasing.

1930 A U.S. Senate investigating committee confirms that church-run boarding schools systematically kidnap Navajo children to meet their quotas.

1935 Navajos vote to reject the Indian Reorganization Act (IRA), refusing to form a U.S.-designed form of government.

1937 The BIA creates a Navajo tribal council to negotiate leases, as large reserves of oil, coal, and natural gas are known to exist on Reservation land.

MAJOR EVENTS IN NAVAJO HISTORY

1942 Navajo code talker program is developed for use in World War II.

1951 Uranium discovered on the Navajo reservation.

1966 Navajo and Hopi tribal councils sign coal-mining leases with coal and copper companies for strip-mining on the newly declared Hopi-Navajo Joint Use Area.

1968 Navajo Code declassified by the U.S. government.

1970 The Mohave Generating Station opens in Nevada, fueled by coal mined on the Navajo and Hopi reservations. The coal leases were known to only a few tribal members. One billion gallons of water per year went into transporting the coal through a pipeline, causing springs to dry up and water levels to drop. Struggles over the water used in the pipeline continue to the present.

1975 Code talkers receive their first national recognition by marching in the New Year's Day Tournament of Roses Parade.

1979 The largest nuclear accident in the United States (including Three Mile Island) occurs at a United Nuclear Company milling plant on the Navajo reservation in New Mexico. More than 100 million gallons of radioactive water pours into the Rio Puerco River through a ruptured dam. Cleanup continues through a Superfund program.

1982 President Ronald Regan declares August 14 as National Navajo Code Talkers Day.

1990 U.S. Congress passes a compensation bill for Navajo uranium miners who had suffered from toxic working conditions for decades.

1992 Pentagon dedicates a new exhibit that honors the code talkers in September.

1996 In a landmark ruling, the Navajo of Black Mesa win a suit against Peabody Coal Company, America's largest coal producer. The suit stated that Peabody's strip-mining operation polluted the air, contaminated groundwater, affected the health of residents, killed livestock, and destroyed Indian burial sites. Peabody was forced to work in compliance with environmental laws. The coal from this site supplies electricity for Phoenix, Los Angeles, and Las Vegas and the power to run the enormous water project, the Central Arizona Project.

2000 In April, Senator Jeff Bingaman (Democrat, New Mexico) introduces legislation to honor the original 29 code talkers with Congressional Gold Medals and all other code talkers with Congressional Silver Medals. In December, Congress passes the "Honoring the Navajo Code Talkers Act," awarding the Congressional Medal to all of World War II's Navajo code talkers.

2001 Navajo Code Talkers' Congressional Medal award ceremony held at the Capitol in Washington, D.C., on July 26. On November 24, 250 Congressional Silver Medals are presented to Navajo code talkers at a ceremony in Window Rock, Arizona.

TODAY The Navajo Reservation is the largest Indian reservation in the United States, covering a total of 17.5 million acres.

Source: Native American History, by Judith Nies, Ballantine Books, 1996.

THIS PAGE: *Navajo men in front of a hogan in Monument Valley, Arizona, 1927.*
PREVIOUS PAGE: *Navajo boy on a horse in Monument Valley circa 1927.*

CAST

Nicolas Cage
as Sergeant Joe Enders

"The character of Yahzee is very innocent, and he doesn't realize when he steps into this war that it's very chaotic, it's a mad house. At one point he becomes a crazy madman lost into this world.... I grew up hearing stories of a decorated Native American soldier named Tommy Prince, and that heroic figure helped me portray a soldier in World War II."
—ADAM BEACH

Adam Beach
as Private Ben Yahzee, Code Talker

"When you're out there on the set and you're seeing people being blown up and shot at, you just really want to make sure it never happens again. And I think John Woo is painting a picture that would scare the hell out of anybody from wanting to make that happen again."
—NICOLAS CAGE

Christian Slater
as Pete "Ox" Anderson

"[Filming Windtalkers] blew all of us away. World War II had truly been re-created. It was epic and massive, and it felt both dangerous and scary to be a part of it."

—CHRISTIAN SLATER

Roger Willie
as Private Charlie Whitehorse, Code Talker

"The movie presents an opportunity for the code talkers and the Navajo people in general to be exposed to the entire world."

—ROGER WILLIE

CAST

Peter Stormare
as Gunnery Sergeant Hjelmstad

Brian Van Holt
as Private Harrigan

Noah Emmerich
as "Chick"

"I love the journey that my character takes in this film. He starts from a place of ignorance with respect to Navajo and moves to a place of real respect and understanding."

—NOAH EMMERICH

Frances O'Connor
as Rita, a WAVE nurse

Martin Henderson
as Private Nellie

Mark Ruffalo
as Private Pappas

Filming Was Brutal

FOR the actors, who did a lot of their own stunts, working in a production designed to reproduce combat as realistically as possible was terrifying at times:

CHRISTIAN SLATER: "It was one dangerous, fear-ridden scene after another. Some of these long scenes had us running through mines and bombs—you had to be very careful what path you chose. It blew all of us away, World War II had truly been recreated. It was epic and massive, and it felt both dangerous and scary to be a part of it."

NOAH EMMERICH: "Through the process of making this movie, I now have a new relationship with the concept of war. I've been as close to war as I ever want to get. There were guys coming at you from every direction, screaming, and you're firing your rifle . . . it was horrifying and intense and you didn't really quite know what had happened until ten minutes after they had called 'Cut!'"

BRIAN VAN HOLT: "It was by far the most physical job I've ever had. The special effects were terrifying, and although we were shooting blanks with ear protection, it felt like real bullets were being fired because of the noise."

ADAM BEACH: "I was a little shell-shocked after my first two days of work." The director was very aware of Beach's reaction and recalled those first days of filming. "Adam Beach had never worked in a big-budget movie before," said John Woo, "and when the troops began to advance and attack, the violence was so real that he got truly frightened. When the shooting stopped he said to me, 'John, it's so violent!' I told him that that is war and war is horrifying and that's what I want to show. Adam was so pure that he couldn't stop shaking!"

On Location:
Hawaii as the South Pacific

THE twenty-week shooting schedule for *Windtalkers* was filmed entirely on location in Hawaii and Southern California. Principal photography began on Monday, August 28, 2000, with the most explosive and vast Saipan battle sequences in the epic drama at a privately owned ranch named Kualoa on the Windward side of the island of Oahu, not far from Honolulu.

Covering approximately 4,500 acres, Kualoa is a fully functioning cattle and recreational ranch currently owned by the John Morgan family. A valley nestled between two jutting mountain ranges on the property, roughly one mile wide and 4.5 miles long, provided the perfect landscape for John Woo to capture the haunting realism of the film's opening battle. Dramatically sweeping up from the sea to the top of a ridge, the valley offered the director 360-degree vistas resembling the Pacific island of Saipan.

Hundreds of films have been shot in Hawaii, known as "Hollywood's Tropical Backlot," and the area chosen for *Windtalkers* makes an excellent match for the Saipan battle area. The Kualoa Ranch's Kaawa Valley was selected because of its stunning photographic appeal, easy access, and the film-friendly attitude of the ranch owners. The Morgan family first bought the property from Hawaii's King Kamehameha III in the mid-1800s, and it is located on a parcel of land—an ahupua'a—that stretches between the mountains and the sea to offer equal amounts of perspective and majesty with mountains that rise to 2000 feet.

The logistics involved in staging the enormity of the film's authentic battle sequences in Hawaii were overwhelming and time-consuming. As many as 700 extras were on set at one time—approximately 500 Marines and 250 Japanese soldiers—all of whom were hired locally. With these numbers added to the production crew of approximately 350, *Windtalkers* became its own battalion with a lunch tent often catering to over 1000 people at a time.

"John Woo is involving the audience completely. They're not being shown war, they're in it."

—SCREENWRITER JOHN RICE

Many of the extras came with some form of military background: former Army or Marine recruits, reservists, or active duty servicemen on leave. On some days, hundreds of men in vintage U.S. Marine wardrobe moved their way up from the sea toward the constructed enemy line: a four-foot trench running the length of the ridge simulating where Japanese soldiers had been dug in over fifty years ago. From the ridge, a clear line of sight of the massive Marine movement, multiple field explosions, tank movement, and gunfire left onlookers breathless.

"It was truly amazing," said screenwriter John Rice, "to see a thousand men in a valley, tanks rolling by, and hundreds of explosions going off in one shot. It was such a thrill as a writer to see so many talented people and actors bringing your story to life." Co-writer Joe Batteer recalled, "When we saw the epic scale of the film on that first day, I remembered our first lunch meeting with John Woo months earlier. He had said with good humor that he saw this film as his *Lawrence of Arabia*. Looking down on that valley for the film's first shot, seeing all the men and explosions, there it was. I have to admit I shed a tear."

Prior to filming, most of the principal cast joined a core group of 62 extras for boot camp where they endured a week of rigorous military training to be indoctrinated as World War II Marines. *Windtalkers* received assistance from the Department of Defense which made Kaneohe Marine Corps Base available for the actors' basic training. Under the tutelage of Sergeant Major Jim Dever, a retired twenty-five-year veteran of the Marine Corps, and his active duty Marine instructors, the cast learned how to walk, talk, and think like Marines. Dever, who served as military advisor on the film, said, "They also learned about the Marine Corps, its history

OPPOSITE: Director John Woo on the set in Kaawa Valley, Hawaii.

"They called me 'General' on the set, and when the filming wrapped they gave me a two-star General's jacket. In many ways we were like a real army, I was so proud to be part of such a group of people."

—DIRECTOR JOHN WOO

and structure, how to handle, load and clean the weapons correctly and how to move on the battlefield like real Marines would have at that time."

"Jim Dever, Tom Williams, Matt Morgan and Dan King were very helpful," said Woo of the film's military experts. "They told me all the details and history of the war from not only the American side but from the Japanese as well. Everything had to be authentic, from the military formations to attack patterns to how to hold and fire a gun. They called me 'General' on the set, and when the filming wrapped they gave me a two-star General's jacket. In many ways we were like a real army, I was so proud to be part of such a group of people."

Boot camp gave the actors a taste of military life, introducing them to the tactical maneuvers, Marine terminology, weapons, and wardrobe of the film. "When I got back from boot camp I watched *Full Metal Jacket*, said Noah Emmerich. The first half of that movie is about boot camp, and I realized how much I had learned—the terminology, phrases and things they were doing were all familiar to

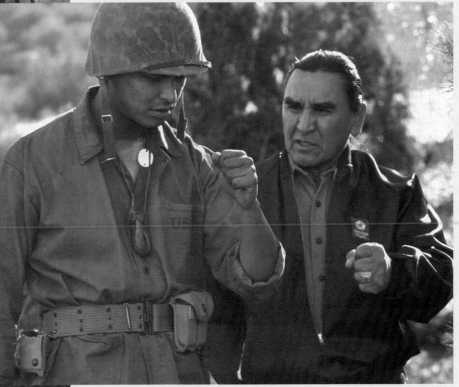

OPPOSITE: *Nicolas Cage in front of the camera.* ABOVE: *Adam Beach gets instruction from spiritual advisor Gilbert Brown.*

me." But perhaps the most important result was that the cast began principal photography on the film as friends, better able to simulate the bond of their characters and impart a sense of realism to their scenes. "We bonded not only with each other," said Brian Van Holt, "but with the rest of the Marines and guys working with us on the movie." Still reeling from the experience of boot camp, the cast arrived on the set in Hawaii with adrenaline pumping, ready for combat.

The authentic Marine and Japanese wardrobes helped to create this sense of realism on the set. Working months in advance from historical resource material, costume supervisor Nick Scarano had 1300 Marine and 1000 Japanese uniforms manufactured from specially selected fabrics. In keeping with Woo's commitment to authenticity, Scarano worked diligently with a crew of textile artists to distress the costumes to look as though they had endured the worst of battle. In doing research, Scarano learned that the uniforms of the Marines in World War II were mismatched. "They were the last of the soldiers to get uniforms," he said, "so they ended up with a mishmash of ill-fitting camouflage and green fatigues."

The chain of command on the set operated much like one would imagine in battle. Woo relayed his vision to his assistant

ABOVE: *John Woo, left, directs Nicolas Cage and Adam Beach in a pivotal scene from the movie.* RIGHT: *Hundreds of extras were used as soldiers in the filming of* Windtalkers.

68

director and right hand man, Arthur Anderson, and to his trusted stunt coordinator Brian Smrz. The physical movement of the vast numbers of extras would then be organized by the military technical advisor, Dever, who would instruct his nine platoon commanders, leading 40-50 men each through squad leaders, on the formation of the men for each take. Authenticity was of paramount concern to Woo, and Dever delivered.

Dispersed amongst these extras were some 40 stunt men, also in military costume, who moved with the men and shielded them from the innumerable explosives rigged by the special effects team. Under the supervision of Smrz, who had worked as stunt coordinator with Woo on his last four films, many of the rugged and highly trained stunt men also ran through fire balls and took numerous "squib hits" while simulating the rigor and violence of combat. Producer Chang noted, "John is a very visual person and his films are very stylized. Even though this film is very realistic in its depic-

tion of war, it will also have his unique stamp on it."

Weapons coordinator Rock Galotti amassed over 500 vintage World War II-era firing weaponry and 700 rubber replica weapons for the film from private collectors and prop houses. The Marines in the film were equipped with M1 rifles, M1 carbines, Browning Automatic rifles, and Thompson sub machine guns, while the Japanese soldiers were armed with Arisaka rifles, Japanese type 92 machine guns, and type 99 light machine guns. Galotti estimated that over half a million rounds of ammunition were used on the film. Also rumbling across the *Windtalkers* battlefields were vintage Sherman tanks, their smaller Stuart brethren, and Japanese Hago tanks.

While the lush greenery of the valley in Oahu made for beautiful images, the frequent tropical showers that imbue the greenery of the landscape with its vibrant color posed logistical difficulties for the production. The rainstorms could be relentless or intermittent, but the effect was the same: mud, knee-high at times. The brown

murk made access roads impossibly dangerous for production vehicles to navigate; numerous pyrotechnic effects were halted and cameras, gear, and wardrobe had to be shielded. Exhausted, drenched, and covered with mud, the crew would often return home to the hotel in Waikiki Beach nearly unrecognizable.

According to the Honolulu Film Office, *Windtalkers* was filmed during weeks of "unusually heavy rains." "We kept losing shooting days because of the rain and the mud," said Woo. "It rained all the time. There was a huge battle scene that we had to film in a valley and it got so muddy that cars kept getting stuck and it was just extremely messy. The weather made shooting very difficult and as a result, we had to cut down on some of the scenes. Fortunately, everyone worked so well together that we got seventy percent of what we needed, which ended up being enough."

When filming was completed at Kualoa Ranch, the production moved to the coconut groves of Dillingham Estate on the North Shore of Oahu to shoot portions of the film's Tipo Pale sequence. This dusty and arid locale, teaming with flies, provided respite for the crew from the rains of Kualoa. After two months of filming on location in Hawaii, the cast and crew of *Windtalkers* relocated to the mainland where they resumed filming in southern California.

Naval Air Weapons Station, Point Mugu, was used to film the Camp Tarawa portion of the film, the Marines pre-battle embarkation point. The Veteran's Administration Hospital in West Los Angeles served as the location for the sequence in which Enders, while recuperating from battle injuries, meets Rita. After a few bitter cold nights of filming in Malibu Creek State Park, the cast and crew moved to a privately owned ranch in the high desert of Los Angeles County for the remaining two months of filming.

ABOVE: John Woo, center left, and Director of Photography Jeffrey L. Kimball, in white, set up one of the many battle sequences.

OPENING FADE IN . . .
Thick fog shrouds an eerie,
dreamlike battlefield on the
Solomon Islands in the Pacific.
A Marine corporal, Joe Enders,
orders his unit to keep fighting
and hold the beachhead, but the
Japanese cut his men down, one
by one. Bodies, blood, and the
death cries of his fellow Marines
rip through Enders' soul. When a
grenade blasts nearby, he sees
a white flash—and this battle
is over.

The Story of the Film

WINDTALKERS is a story of war, but it is also a tale of men from different cultures and backgrounds bridging those contrasts through friendship, trust, and the harrowing experience of battle. Amidst the horror of war, an indomitable bond develops between the code talkers and their fellow Marines. Their friendships and Marine duty are put to the test in the face of explosive artillery warfare, sniper attacks, fallen comrades, and excruciating morale dilemmas.

"*Windtalkers* is about a topic that I'm always looking for," said director John Woo. "It's about two different people from two different cultures who grow from each other while they learn to work together. Since I come from the East, I feel I have a personal mission. I see myself as a bridge, bringing two cultures together in order to make people understand each other better.

"I wanted the message of the film to be anti-war," Woo continued. "I wanted to let people see that war only damages our world and that the only contribution the human race can make is friendship. The movie is about redemption and the need to care."

The title of the film reflects the code talkers themselves as well as their Navajo heritage. "The wind is very important in the Navajo scheme of things," explained screenwriter John Rice. "It's true to their creation myths. It also feels ethereal, and we wanted to imbue the piece with a kind of spirituality. Our piece is about a man, Joe Enders, who has been thrown out of balance by war, and the spiritual and inner healing that goes on within him."

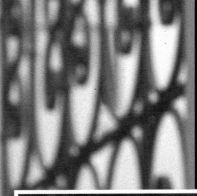

...Enders wakes up in a field hospital and is presented with the Purple Heart for bravery in battle. But the medal is no consolation for a man who has witnessed his men falling, suffering, and dying under his command. Enders' damaged eardrum has a chance of healing, but the wounds that lie deep in his psyche threaten to haunt him forever.

SCENE: MONUMENT VALLEY, ARIZONA. A young Navajo, Ben Yahzee, says goodbye to his wife and son as he boards the bus that will take he and his friend, Charlie Whitehorse, to training camp where they will learn the top-secret military code based on their native language.

"Ben Yahzee is a hard man not to like," said screenwriter Rice. "He's a man who has a deep, abiding respect for all aspects of life, and war hasn't yet polluted him." As they watch their sacred land rush past, Yahzee and Whitehorse leave their old lives—their innocent, sheltered lives—behind. "Yahzee wants to go to war to serve his country," added Rice. "He wants to be like the braves in his nation that used to go to war. But maybe he isn't quite ready for the horror of war and the bloodletting and all that he'll see." Yahzee has been outside the Reservation and seen some of the world. "He is learned, smart and wants to go and make a big name for himself," said Rice. "He believes in the American melting pot theory." Whitehorse, a practicing medicine man who carries a leather medicine pouch and traditional flute, is not as trusting as his younger friend. "Our other Navajo character, Whitehorse, is much more skeptical of the white man," said Rice. "He's a man who hasn't seen as much but has an inner knowing."

ABOVE: Navajo code talkers in formation at Camp Elliot, California, circa 1942.

SCENE: A MILITARY OFFICE.
Enders, out of the hospital and ready to get back into action in the Pacific, receives his new orders from Major Mellitz. He is to team up with and protect a code talker—a Navajo trained to communicate field orders in a top-secret code based on his native language. Not only is Enders expected to keep his code talker alive so he can do his job, he is also ordered to safeguard the code at all costs. The no-nonsense major explains that, should the code talker face capture by the enemy, Enders is to protect the code, not the man. He must be prepared to kill a fellow Marine.

MAJOR MELLITZ
Corporal, what I'm about to tell
you is not to leave this room. Under
no circumstances can you allow
your Codetalker to fall into enemy
hands. Your mission is to protect
the code . . . at all costs.

SCENE: CAMP TARAWA, HOME OF THE MARINES OF THE 2ND DIVISION. Enders joins up with his new unit, which includes Pete "Ox" Anderson, another sergeant ordered to bodyguard duty; Pappas, a Greek American; Chick, a cocky Texan; Harrigan, a Californian with hair bleached from days on Daytona Beach; and Nellie, a newlywed.

When the two Navajo code talkers—the unit's radio specialists—roll into camp, Ox eyes them curiously but Enders doesn't appear interested. He had made friends with fellow soldiers before, and their deaths still ripped him apart inside. Enders would not put himself through the same agony again.

Ox throws a card to Harrigan, hair bleached from days on Daytona Beach, firing a new smoke from a dying one.

OX
Another mess for the Sunshine State. (deals his own card, smiles) And a third nine for the dealer.

Harrigan eyes his hole cards, tosses out a quarter.

HARRIGAN
Two bits. (turns to Chick) And you ain't gotta worry about sitting on your butt much longer, got a buddy in Intelligence says we're shipping out next week.

CHICK
Shit... . Been hearing next week for a month.

NELLIE (puts on a smile)
Next year'd be alright with me.

PAPPAS (still eyeing Harrigan)
You got a friend in Intelligence, Hairy?

Everyone bets, the pot's right. Cards come down, Enders' last. Full house, kings and queens.

ENDERS
Cowboys over queens, read 'em and die.

Murmurs of disgust. Pappas stands, has seen Enders rake in enough pots.

PAPPAS
Fuck it. I'm done.

Nellie, eyes his holdings, twists at the wedding band on his finger.

NELLIE
Yeah, better go write the missus. (forces a laugh) God knows what a girl'll do without reassurance.

The others stay their ground. Ox looks over to Yahzee and Whitehorse.

OX
Hey, we could use some new blood, gentlemen, come play some cards.

83

Gunnery Sergeant Hjelmstad briefs the unit on their duties as the reconnaissance force, and tells them that they'll ship out for "paradises unknown" the next day.

"The code talker," said Rice, "is a man who Joe Enders doesn't want to get to know, doesn't want to become friendly with. He's made friends at war before, and they're taken from him." At the outdoor luau that night, Enders has a drink with the WAVE nurse, Rita, who helped him recover at the field hospital. With loud young Marines celebrating all around them, they slip out for a drive to the beach.

SCENE: SAIPAN, MARIANA ISLAND, JUNE 16, 1944. Enders and his unit join the massive Marine offensive onto the island, advancing into hilly terrain that explodes with Japanese cannon shells, mortars, and machine-gun and rifle fire. In the smoky air above, Hellcats drop 250-pound bombs on Japanese weapons bunkers. Young code talker Yahzee is stunned by the blood, carnage, explosions, choking smoke, and screams of dying men. Staying close to Enders, he witnesses what machine gun fire from an enemy Hago tank can do to a man. On Enders' orders, he presses his hand onto a soldier's crimson chest wound to try to stop the bleeding. U.S. Stuart tanks fire their 37mm cannons at the Hago tanks and the fireballs incinerate the enemy soldiers inside.

Yahzee puts the code into practice for the first time when Enders shouts a group of coordinates to him to relay to the battleships offshore. *Target reference dog one, right seven hundred. Elevation one five zero.* Yahzee has a tight squeeze on the radio but hesitates, watching in horror as a Marine gets shot down just a few feet in front of him. Enders yells at him to relay the orders, and the code talker shakes off the image and begins to speak into the phone. The first hit reveals that the coordinates were slightly short of their target, but seconds after Yahzee relays the new transmission a volcanic-sized explosion rips through the target: a Japanese machine-gun bunker. Meanwhile, Japanese radiomen listen in on the Marine transmissions and try to match up the words in their American code books. It's evidently code, but it's unlike anything they've ever heard. Without the ability to decipher the messages, their cannons and bunkered soldiers are sitting ducks for pinpointed American fire.

YAHZEE
Arizona, Arizona . . .
(subtitled Navajo)
Request fire mission . . .

JAPANESE RADIOMAN
Sounds like they are
underwater. English?

INTELLIGENCE OFFICER
(listens, shakes his head)
. . . No. It's code.

91

When the fighting ends, Yahzee, Whitehorse, and other Marines stare down from their hard-won hilltop, surveying a battlefield littered with corpses. Later that night Whitehorse turns to Yahzee and performs an Evilway, a traditional ceremony to protect his friend from the spirits of the dead that surround them. He smears ash on Yahzee's cheeks and dabs corn pollen—taken from the deer-skin pouch that dangles from his neck—onto Yahzee's forehead. *I saw you a warrior, Yahzee. You will make our people proud.*

YAHZEE
It's called an Evilway. (off Enders' look) What you saw Charlie doing to me. Navajo believe until a body's given proper burial, the spirit stays near it. Chendis, that's what we call evil spirits. I haven't thought much about any of that since I was a kid. . . until I saw all those dead guys. . .

SCENE: A QUIET STREAM IN THE EARLY MORNING. Yahzee bathes in a peaceful oasis, his uniform hanging on a branch nearby. Chick and Pappas find him, and Chick starts a fight, letting his prejudice about Native Americans rear up and overtake his respect for the Corps. When Enders rushes in to break it up, Chick covers up his intention with the excuse that he mistook Yahzee for a Japanese soldier.

94

CHICK
Ben? . . . thought it was a Nip killed
some Marine for that uniform.

ENDERS
Sure you did, Chick.

CHICK
Well he does, don't he? Damn Injun looks
just like a Nip.

YAHZEE
(grabs up his clothes) I'm not a damn
Injun, I'm Navajo. Of the Bitter Water
People, born for the Towering House Clan.

"We have one character in our movie who is prejudiced," said Rice. "I think there's a certain prejudice in the orders themselves, too, that you may have to kill this Navajo. It hearkens back to the days when we'd make a treaty and then fudge the treaty, saying to the Indians, in effect, 'we're not going to tell you everything.' And in this film there's a certain amount that wasn't known to the Navajo."

During the war in the Pacific, the Navajo were sometimes mistaken for Japanese by the enemy as well as by their fellow Marines. In the next scene, Yahzee devises a way to turn this to the unit's advantage. When the squads come under friendly fire, Yahzee's radio is hit and blown to smithereens. He has no way to notify American forces that they are blowing up their own convoy—except to get to another radio. Yahzee pulls the uniform off a dead Japanese body and convinces Enders and Hjelmstad to let him infiltrate the enemy area. It's their only chance of finding a radio and calling in the information. Enders refuses to let him go alone, and they quickly come up with a plan to pose as a Japanese scout and his Marine prisoner. The risky operation works—and Yahzee undergoes a baptism of blood when he plunges his bayonet into an enemy soldier at the radio position. After calling in the message and new coordinates, Yahzee looks up to see the firing change course and take out the Japanese unit they had just marched through.

YAHZEE
Horyo!

Yahzee gives Enders a shove, moves him through the trench line. . . The Japanese look at Yahzee, CURSE him for not checking for weapons. . .

JAPANESE SERGEANT (subtitled):
What unit are you?!

Yahzee knows the voice is directed at him, just walks faster.

Ox and his code talker, Whitehorse, are growing closer, too. During breaks from battle, Ox pulls out his harmonica and makes music with Whitehorse, who serenades on his flute. At another end of the camp, Enders finally opens up and tells Yahzee about the day on the beachhead when he watched his three friends and many more in his unit die. Yahzee tells him it wasn't his fault, that he was just following orders. But he can see the pain in his bodyguard's eyes and hear it in his voice. When Enders appears to have passed out from exhaustion and alcohol, Yahzee gently rubs a smear of ash onto his forehead. This is a Protectionway, a ritual for healing and safety.

SCENE: CHARAN KANOA, A BATTERED VILLAGE. The air roars with smoke and flame as the first and second squads battle the Japanese near the gutted remains of a Buddhist temple.

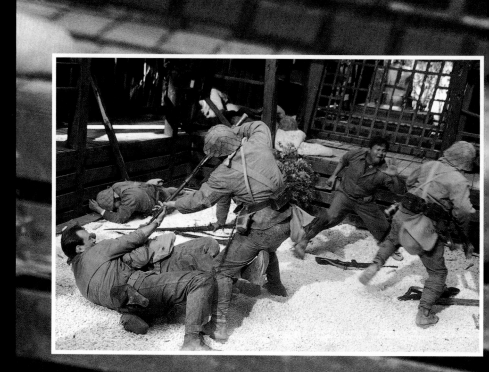

The moment Enders has feared arrives when he discovers that Whitehorse is badly wounded and vulnerable to capture. The code talker's bodyguard, Ox, lies dead on a bloody street. To Enders' horror, a Japanese soldier has found Whitehorse and is aiming his rifle, ready to kill. But before he can pull the trigger a Japanese intelligence officer recognizes that Whitehorse may be a Navajo code talker and orders him taken alive. As the officer moves quickly toward Whitehorse, Enders grabs a hand grenade from his belt. He throws it at the cluster of Japanese who have now picked up Whitehorse and are leading him away. Enders has his orders—protect the code at all costs.

ENDERS
Na-nil-in. . . You know what it means,
Private. Something kept secret.

YAHZEE
. . . What're you talking about?

ENDERS
My orders. (shakes his head) You
Codetalkers are important, that's why
they stuck me on your ass. . . but
nobody's as important as the code.
Japanese got hold of a Codetalker,
Codetalker talks, code's useless. I
didn't have a choice. My order's to
protect the code.

SCENE: A MINE FIELD LEADING TO A HIGH JUNGLE SLOPE. Hardened by battle and the death of his friend, Yahzee plunges fearlessly through a mine field, weaving a safe path for the unit that follows behind. Filled with hatred, rage, and the need to kill, he blasts away at the enemy as Enders furiously tries to keep up and cover him. In a flash, Yahzee is hit by enemy fire in the stomach and both legs. He is immobilized and vulnerable as the enemy quickly moves in.

Enders, who has dragged Pappas to safety while covering Yahzee, finds his code talker badly wounded. With the enemy surrounding them, Enders is faced with the order to protect the code—and kill the code talker. Yahzee is now fully resigned to his fate and explains to Enders that it's all right to kill him because he knows that the code is more important than his own life. Enders aims his rifle—but suddenly changes his mind and lifts Yahzee over his shoulder to make a run for safety. He dives into a trench and covers Yahzee with his body to protect him from the bullets that rain around them. In his act as a human shield, Enders is severely wounded.

Enders spends his last moments sharing his thoughts about war and humanity with Yahzee, who holds his dying bodyguard in his arms. The two men have developed a bond of friendship that will link them forever. With a look of hard-won peace on his face, Enders breathes his last breath and leaves his code talker, his unit, and the world behind.

SCENE: MONUMENT VALLEY, UTAH. Yahzee, his wife, and son, dressed in traditional Navajo dress, are sitting atop a rock outcropping with a campfire.

YAHZEE
His name was Joe Enders from South Philadelphia. He was a fierce warrior, a good Marine. (turns to his son) If you ever tell a story about him, George, say he was my friend.

Ultimate Tributes:
The Congressional Medal Ceremonies, 2001

ON July 26, 2001, the crowd in the Capitol Rotunda in Washington, D.C., gave a rousing standing ovation to four special World War II veterans as they made their way to the podium. The honorees—four of the five living Navajo code talkers—would in moments be presented the Congressional Gold Medal from President George W. Bush for their service in the war.

Congress passed the "Honoring the Navajo Code Talkers Act" based on legislation written by U.S. Senator Jeff Bingaman of New Mexico. The act was signed into law—Public Law No. 106-554—by President Bill Clinton on December 21, 2000. This law awarded Congressional Medals to all of World War II's Navajo code talkers.

The 29 Navajo code talkers who developed the code were awarded with gold medals, and the approximately 400 Navajo who

> **Five Living Navajo Code Talkers**
> **as of September 2001**
>
> John Brown, Jr.
> Allen Dale June
> Chester Nez
> Lloyd Oliver
> Joe Palmer (*could not attend ceremony*)

later qualified as code talkers during the war were awarded silver medals. Although most of the medals have been awarded posthumously, they signify the highest civilian honor Congress can bestow upon a specific individual, organization, or event. Established during the American Revolution, the medals are given as an expression of national appreciation for distinguished achievements and contributions. To be awarded, medals must be co-sponsored by 67 Senators and at least two-thirds of the members of the House. Each medal is specifically designed for the recipient (or group of recipients), and the Secretary of the Treasury is the final judge of the design. The medals are made at the U.S. Mint in Philadelphia.

"These medals are to express recognition by the United States of America and its citizens of the Navajo Code Talkers," said Senator Bingaman, "who distinguished themselves in performing a unique, highly successful communications operation that greatly assisted in saving countless lives and in hastening the end of World War II in the Pacific Theater. It has taken too long to properly recognize these soldiers, whose achievements have been obscured by twin veils of secrecy and time. As they approach the final chapter of their lives, it is only fitting that the nation pay them this honor. That's why I introduced this legislation—to salute these brave and innovative Native Americans, to acknowledge the great contribution they made to the Nation at a time of war, and to finally give them their rightful place in history."

Addressing the crowd, the Senator said, "Their story is known by some but not by enough, and this ceremony today gives them the recognition they have long deserved.

LEFT: *Navajo code talker John Brown, Jr., at the Congressional Gold Medal award ceremony in Washington, D.C.*

The Navajo Nation is a very important part of New Mexico, always has been and always will be, and there's no accomplishment by the Navajo people that they're more proud of than the work that the code talkers did in the Second World War."

In an earlier statement about the code talkers, Senator Bingaman said, "The code was so successful that the Department of Defense kept the Code secret for 23 years after the end of World War II, when it was finally declassified in 1968. If their achievements had been hailed at the conclusion of the war, proper honors would have been bestowed at that time. But the Code Talkers were sworn to secrecy, an oath they kept and honored, but at the same time, one that robbed them of the very accolades and place in history they so rightly deserved."

During the ceremony, code talker John Brown, Jr., said, "It is indeed an honor to be here today before you representing my fellow distinguished Navajo code talkers. Only destiny has demanded my presence here."

President Bush presented the medals to Brown, Allen Dale June, Chester Nez, and Lloyd Oliver, and in his speech stated, "In presenting gold medals to each of them, the Congress recognizes their individual service, bravely offered and flawlessly performed."

Windtalkers director John Woo and actors Nicolas Cage, Adam Beach, and Roger Willie also attended the stirring tribute. "The ceremony was very moving and beautiful," said Woo. "It really touched my heart and I was honored to be a part of it."

"I wanted to pay my respects to the heroes who were honored today," Cage said just after the ceremony, "and I thought it was important that the filmmakers participate in it as well. I thought it was very emotional to see this honor finally bestowed upon them after quite a bit of time and, from my perspective, it seemed like a weight had been taken off these gentlemen."

Awarding the remaining hundreds of code talkers with silver medals would take a larger space than the Capitol Rotunda. On Saturday, November 24, 2001, 250 Congressional Silver Medals were presented in a three-hour ceremony on the Navajo Nation Fairgrounds in Window Rock, Arizona. Neil McCaleb of the Bureau of Indian Affairs presented the medals to the largest group ever to receive the honor. Some of the elderly honorees wore the gold velveteen shirt and red cap that make up the uniform of the Navajo Code Talkers Association while others wore red silk U.S. Marine Corps jackets. Whether walking single file or rolling up the aisle of Nakal Hall in wheelchairs, the code talkers met McCaleb one-by-one, in alphabetical order, to receive the medals that recognize their achievements and contributions to World War II. The ceremony included a moving version of the National

ABOVE: Nicolas Cage signing the guest book at the Capitol Rotunda ceremony. LEFT: Senator Jeff Bingaman, who wrote the legislation awarding Congressional Medals to the code talkers, speaking at the Gold Medal award ceremony.

> *"Just 77 years before World War II the grandfathers of these men were forced at gunpoint with 9,000 other people [to walk] 300 miles. For these men to rise above that injustice speaks of great courage, great patriotism. Americans owe these great men a debt of gratitude."*
>
> —SENATOR BEN NIGHTHORSE (COLORADO), SPEAKING AT THE GOLD MEDAL CEREMONY

Anthem sung in Navajo by a group of family members of Navajo code talkers, and the Navajo Nation band also performed.

The Marine Corps had not yet completed the official certification process in naming all the code talkers who served in the war; therefore, additional medals are scheduled to be awarded when all the recipients are verified. Less than half of the code talkers are still living, and the medals of those who have died are presented to surviving family members. Without a central file on the code talkers, the Marine Corps has had to search millions of files to find documentation that confirms which men served as code talkers. Officials also asked family members of deceased code talkers to send any records they could find to help verify that their relative was an authentic code talker.

On hand at the Silver Medal ceremony to congratulate the code talkers were U.S. Representative Tom Udall of New Mexico, Navajo President Kelsey A. Begaye, Navajo Nation Council Speaker Edward T. Begay, and New Mexico State senators Albert Tom, Sylvia Laughter, and John Pinto. When they reached the stage, the code talkers each received a salute from Brigadier General Kathy Thomas. "What you have done, the sacrifices you made, have protected our freedom and allowed us all to 'Walk in Beauty,'" she said to the group, referring to the Navajo philosophy of life. President Kelsey, a Vietnam War veteran, added, "You leave a legacy we have never truly filled. From this day forward we will continue to remember the courage and sacrifice of the Navajo Code Talkers. You are our true American heroes."

U.S. Marine Corps List of Navajo Code Talkers Verified as of November 2001

The certification process is ongoing and the U.S. Marines anticipate the addition of approximately 60 names.

Dan Akee	Samuel Billison	Tully Davis
Franklin Anthony	Sam Billy	Martin Deel
Jimmie Apache	Wilfred Billy	Dan Debiya
Bennie Arviso	Wilsie Bitsie	Leo Dennison
Regis Ashley	Peter Bitsie	George Dennison
Earl Ashike	Delford Bitsoi	James Dixon
Harold Attikai	Jesse Bizardie	Jerome Dodge
John Augustine	Jesse Black	John Doolie
Lewis Ayze	Paul Blatchford	Richardson Doolie
Henry Bahe, Jr.	David Bluehorse	Nelson Draper
Woody Bahe	John Bowman	Teddy Draper, Sr.
Benjamin Baldwin	Robert Bowman	Kee Etsicitty
Harold Beard	Arthur Brown	Deswood Etsitty
Roy Bercenti	Clarence Brown	Harold Evans
Sidney Bedoni	Cosey S. Brown	Ray Foghorn
Carlos Begay	John Brown, Jr.	Jimmy Francisco
Charles Begay	Tsosie Brown	Joe Gatewood
Charlie Begay	William Brown	William George
Flemming Begay	Wilford Buck	Milton Gishal
George Begay	Jose Bunnie, Jr.	Jimmie Gleason
Henry Begay	Bobby Burke	John Goodluck
Jerry Begay	Sandy Burr	Carl Gorman
Joe Begay	William Cadman	Tom Gorman
Lee Begay	Andrew Calleditto	Bill Grayson
Leo Begay	Oscar Carroll	Yazzie Greymountain
Leonard Begay	Dennis Cattle Chaser	Billy Guarito
Notah Begay	Del Cayedito	Tully Gustine
Paul Begay	Ralph Cayedito	Charles Guy
Roy Begay	Carson Charley	Leslie Hamstreet
Samuel Begay	Sam Charlie	Ben Harding
Thomas Begay	Frederick Chase	Jack Harding
Walter Begay	George Chavez	Tom Hardy
Willie Begay	Guy Chee	Emmett Harrison
Wilson Begay	John Chee	Ross Haskie
David Begody	Stewart Clah	Roy Hathorne
Rodger Begody	Thomas Claw	Bud Haycock
Wilmer Belinda	Ned Cleveland	Albert Henry
Harry Belone	Ben Cleveland	Edmund Henry
Jimmy Benallie	Billie Cleveland	Kent Henry
Harrison Benally	Leslie Cody	Dean Hickman
Harry Benally	James Cohoe	Calvin Holiday
Jimmie Benally	Bob Craig	Samuel Holiday
John Benally	Eugene Crawford	Johnson Housewood
Johnson Benally	Karl Crawford	Dennie Housteen
Samuel Benally	Walter Cronemeyer	Ambrose Howard
Willie Benton, Sr.	Billy Crosby	Arthur Hubbard
John Bernard	Carl Csinnjinni	Lewey Hudson
Lloyd Betone	David Curley	Tom Hunter
Andrew Bia	Ray Dale	Oscar Ilthma
Ben Billie	Anson Damon	Benjamin James
Howard Billiman	Lowell Damon	Billie James

114

Above: Navajo Code Talkers (left to right) Harold Evans, W. Oliva, and Samuel Smith hold their hands over their hearts as the National Anthem is sung in Navajo at the Congressional Silver Medal Ceremony on November 24, 2001, in Window Rock, Arizona.

George James
Elliott Johle
Edmund Johns
Charlie John
Leroy John
Earl Johnny
Francis Johnson
Johnnie Johnson
Peter Johnson
Deswood Johnson
Ralph Johnson
Tom Jones
Jack Jones
David Jordan
Allen June
Floyd June
Percy Keams
Wilson Keedah
Joe Kellwood
Alonzo Kescoli
Bahe Ketchum
Jimmy King
Paul Kinlaheheeny
John Kinsel
Leo Kirk
George Kirk
Mike Kiyanni
Rex Kontz

Harrison Lapahie
James Largo
Alfred Leonard
Keith Little
Tommie Lopez
Rex Malone
Robert Malone
Max Malone
James Maloney
Paul Maloney
Benjamin Manuelito
Ira Manuelito
James Manuelito
Johnny Manuelito
Peter Manuelito
Frank Marianato
Robert Mark
Matthew Martin
Jose Martinez
William McCabe
Archibald McCraith
King Mike
General Miles
Tom Moffit
Jack Morgan
Ralph Morgan
Joe Morris
George Moss

Calvin Murphy
Oscar Mutine
Martin Napa
Adoph Nagurski
James Nahkai, Jr.
Peter Nakaidinae
Harding Negale
Alfred Newman
Arthur Nez
Chester Nez
Freland Nez
Israel Nez
Jack Nez
Sidney Nez
Roy Notah
Willie Notah
Billy O'dell
Lloyd Oliver
Willard Oliver
Layton Paddock
Robert Pahe
Paul Parrish
Amos Patrick
Alfred Peaches
Sam Peshlakai
Frank Pete
Joe Peterson
Gaul Pinto
John Pinto
Richard Platero
Jimmie Preston
Sam Reed
Harry Roanhorse
Andy Sage
Denny Sage
Jerry Salabiye
Peter Sandoval

Samuel Sandoval
Thomas Sandoval
John Scott
John Sells
Freddie Shields
Dooley Shorty
Robert Shorty
Joe Silversmith
Sammy Silversmith
Oscar Singer
Richard Singer
Wilson Skeet
Richard Slinky
Balmer Slowtalker
  (a.k.a. Joe Palmer)
Albert Silvers
Arcenio Smiley
Albert Smith
George Smith
Raymond Smith
Samual Smith
George Soce
Benjamin Sorrel
Harry Spencer
Johnnie Tabaha
Alfred Tah
Edward Tah
John Talley
Bert Tallsalt
Edward Thomas
Richard Thomas, Sr.
Clare Thompson
Everrett Thompson
Francis Thompson
Frank Thompson
Nelson Thompson
Carl Todacheene

Frank Todacheene
Benson Tohe
Curtis Toledo
Frank Toledo
Preston Toledo
Willie Toledo
Joseph Towne
Zane Towne
Chester Tso
Howard Tso
Paul Tso
Samuel Tso
Alfred Tsosie
Cecil Tsosie
Collins Tsosie
Harry Tsosie
Kenneth Tsosie
Samuel Tsosie, Sr.
John Upshaw
William Upshaw
Joe Vandever
Oliver Wagner
Stephen Wallace
Robert Walley
John Werito

Lyman Whitman
Frank Willeto
Frankie Willeto
Kenneth William
Alex Williams
George Willie
John Willie, Jr.
Clarence Woodty
Ernest Yazhe
Harrison Yazhe
Peter Yazza
Vincent Yazza
Clifton Yazzie
Daniel Yazzie
Eddie Yazzie
Edison Yazzie
Felix Yazzie
Francis Yazzie
Frank Yazzie
Harding Yazzie
Harold Yazzie
Joe Yazzie
John Yazzie
Justin Yazzie
Lemuel Yazzie
Ned Yazzie
Pahe Yazzie
Raphael Yazzie
Robert Yazzie
William Yazzie
Leon Yellowhair
Stanley Yellowhair
Howard Yellowman
George Yoe
Henry Zah

Source: Office of Senator Jeff Bingaman.

Symbolism of the Navajo Code Talkers Association Uniform

Red cap	U.S. Marine Corps
Silver and turquoise jewelry	The Diné
Gold shirt	Corn Pollen
Patches	Six U.S. Marine Divisions
Light-colored trousers	Mother Earth
Abalone-colored shoes	Four Sacred Mountains

The Navajo Code Talker Dictionary

WORD	NAVAJO WORD	LITERAL TRANSLATION	WORD	NAVAJO WORD	LITERAL TRANSLATION
A	Wol-la-chee	Ant	R	Gah	Rabbit
A	Be-la-sana	Apple	R	Dah-nes-tsa	Ram
A	Tse-nill	Axe	R	Ah-losz	Rice
B	Na-hash-chid	Badger	S	Dibeh	Sheep
B	Shush	Bear	S	Klesh	Snake
B	Toish-jeh	Barrel	T	D-ah	Tea
C	Moasi	Cat	T	A-woh	Tooth
C	Tla-gin	Coal	T	Than-zie	Turkey
C	Ba-goshi	Cow	U	Shi-da	Uncle
D	Be	Deer	U	No-da-ih	Ute
D	Chindi	Devil	V	A-keh-di-glini	Victor
D	Lha-cha-eh	Dog	W	Gloe-ih	Weasel
E	Ah-jah	Ear	X	Al-na-as-dzoh	Cross
E	Dzeh	Elk	Y	Tsah-as-zih	Yucca
E	Ah-nah	Eye	Z	Besh-do-tliz	Zinc
F	Chuo	Fir			
F	Tsa-e-donin-ee	Fly			
F	Ma-e	Fox			

NAMES OF VARIOUS ORGANIZATIONS

WORD	NAVAJO WORD	LITERAL TRANSLATION
G	Ah-tad	Girl
G	Klizzie	Goat
G	Jeha	Gum
H	Tse-gah	Hair
H	Cha	Hat
H	Lin	Horse
I	Tkin	Ice
I	Yeh-hes	Itch
I	A-chi	Intestine

Corps	Din-neh-ih	Clan
Division	Ashih-hi	Salt
Regiment	Tabaha	Edge water
Battalion	Tacheene	Red soil
Company	Nakia	Mexican
Platoon	Has-clish-nih	Mud
Section	Yo-ih	Beads
Squad	Debeh-li-zini	Black sheep

OFFICERS

J	Tkele-cho-g	Jackass
J	Ah-ya-tsinne	Jaw
J	Yil-doi	Jerk
K	Jad-ho-loni	Kettle
K	Ba-ah-ne-di-tinin	Key
K	Klizzie-yazzie	Kid
L	Dibeh-yazzie	Lamb
L	Ah-jad	Leg
L	Nash-doie-tso	Lion
M	Tsin-tliti	Match
M	Be-tas-tni	Mirror
M	Na-as-tso-si	Mouse
N	Tsah	Needle
N	A-chin	Nose

Commanding gen.	Bih-keh-he (g)	War chief
Major gen.	So-na-kih	Two star
Brigadier gen.	So-a-la-ih	One star
Colonel	Atsah-besh-le-gai	Silver eagle
Lt. Colonel	Che-chil-be-tah-besh-legai	Silver oak leaf
Major	Che-chil-be-tah-ola	Gold oak leaf
Captain	Besh-legai-nah-kih	Two silver bars
Lieutenant	Besh-legai-a-lah-ih	One silver bar
Commanding officer	Hash-kay-gi-na-tah	War chief
Executive officer	Bih-da-hol-nehi	Those in charge

O	A-kha	Oil
O	Tlo-chin	Onion
O	Ne-ahs-jah	Owl

NAMES OF COUNTRIES

P	Cla-gi-aih	Pant
P	Bi-so-dih	Pig
P	Ne-zhoni	Pretty
Q	Ca-yeilth	Quiver

Africa	Zhin-ni	Blackies
Alaska	Beh-hga	With winter
America	Ne-he-mah	Our mother
Australia	Cha-yes-desi	Rolled hat
Britain	Toh-ta	Between waters
China	Ceh-yehs-besi	Braided hair

WORD	NAVAJO WORD	LITERAL TRANSLATION	WORD	NAVAJO WORD	LITERAL TRANSLATION
France	Da-gha-hi	Beard	October	Nil-chi-tsosie	Small wind
Germany	Besh-be-cha-he	Iron hat	November	Nil-chi-tso	Big wind
Iceland	Tkin-ke-yah	Ice land	December	Yas-nil-tes	Crusted snow
India	Ah-le-gai	White clothes			
Italy	Doh-ha-chi-yali-tchi	Stutter	**VOCABULARY**		
Japan	Beh-na-ali-tsosie	Slant eye	Abandon	Ye-tsan	Run away from
Philippines	Ke-yah-da-na-lhe	Floating island	About	Wola-chi-a-moffa-gahn	Ant fight
Russia	Sila-gol-chi-ih	Red army	Abreast	Wola-chee-be-yied	Ant breast
South america	Sha-de-ah-ne-hi-mah	South our mother	Accomplish	Ul-so	All done
Spain	Deba-de-nih	Sheep pain	According	Be-ka-ho	According to
			Acknowledge	Hanot-dzied	Acknowledge
NAMES OF AIRPLANES			Action	Ah-ha-tinh	Place of action
Planes	Wo-tah-de-ne-ih	Air force	Activity	Ah-ha-tinh-y	Action ending in Y
Dive bomber	Gini	Chicken hawk	Adequate	Beh-gha	Enough
Torpedo plane	Tas-chizzie	Swallow	Addition	Ih-he-de-ndel	Addition
Obs. plan	Ne-as-jah	Owl	Address	Yi-chin-ha-tse	Address
Fighter plane	Da-he-tih-hi	Humming bird	Adjacent	Be-gahi	Near
Bomber plane	Jay-sho	Buzzard	Adjust	Has-tai-nel-kad	Adjust
Patrol plane	Ga-gih	Crow	Advance	Nas-sey	Ahead
Transport	Atsah	Eagle	Advise	Na-netin	Advise
			Aerial	Be-zonz	Stinger
NAMES OF SHIPS			Affirmative	Lanh	Affirmative
Ships	Toh-dineh-ih	Sea force	After	Bi-kha-di (a)	After
Battleship	Lo-tso	Whale	Against	Be-na-gnish	Against
Aircraft	Tsidi-moffa-ye-hi	Bird carrier	Aid	Eda-ele-tsood	Aid
Submarine	Besh-lo	Iron fish	Air	Nilchi	Air
Mine sweeper	Cha	Beaver	Airdome	Nilchi-beghan	Airdome
Destroyer	Ca-lo	Shark	Alert	Ha-ih-des-ee	Alert
Transport	Dineh-nay-ye-hi	Man carrier	All	Ta-a-tah (a)	All
Cruiser	Lo-tso-yazzie	Small whale	Allies	Nih-hi-cho	Allies
Mosquito boat	Tse-e	Mosquito	Along	Wolachee-snez	Long ant
			Also	Eh-do	Also
			Alternate	Na-kee-go-ne-nan-dey-he	Second position

June: Big planting

WORD	NAVAJO WORD	LITERAL TRANSLATION
NAMES OF MONTHS		
January	Atsah-be-yaz	Small eagle
February	Woz-cheind	Squeaky voice
March	Tah-chill	Small plant
April	Tah-tso	Big plant
May	Tah-tsosie	Small plant
June	Be-ne-eh-eh-jah-tso	Big planting
July	Be-ne-ta-tsosie	Small harvest
August	Be-neen-ta-tso	Big harvest
September	Ghaw-jih	Half

WORD	NAVAJO WORD	LITERAL TRANSLATION
Ambush	khac-da	Ambush
Ammunition	beh-eli-doh-be-cah-ali-tas-ai	Ammunition
Amphibious	Chal	Frog
And	Do	And
Angle	Dee-cahn	Slanting
Annex	ih-nay-tani	Addition
Announce	beh-ha-o-dze	Announce
Anti	wol-la-chee-tsin	Ant ice
Anticipate	Ni-jol-lih	Anticipate
Any	Tah-ha-dah	Any
Appear	Ye-ka-ha-ya	Appear

America: Our mother

WORD	NAVAJO WORD	LITERAL TRANSLATION	WORD	NAVAJO WORD	LITERAL TRANSLATION
Approach	Bi-chi-ol-dah	Approach	Cable	Besh-lkoh	Wire rope
Approximate	To-kus-dan	Approximate	Caliber	Nahl-kihd	Move around
Are	Gah-tso big	Rabbit	Camp	To-altseh-hogan	Temporary place
Area	Haz-a-gih	Area	Camouflage	Di-nes-ih	Hid
Armor	Besh-ye-ha-da-di-teh	Iron protector	Can	Yah-di-zini	Can
Army	Lei-cha-ih-yil-knee-ih	Army	Cannon	Eerbe-al-doh-tso-dey-dil-don-igi	Big gun operator
Arrive	Il-day	Arrive	Capacity	Be-nel-ah	Capacity
Artillery	Be-al-doh-tso-lani	Many big guns	Capture	Yis-nah	Capture
As	Ahce	As	Carry	Yo-lailh	Carry
Assault	Altseh-e-jah-he	First striker	Case	Bit-sah	Case
Assemble	De-ji-kash	Bunch together	Casualty	Bih-din-ne-dey	Put out of action
Assign	Bah-deh-tahn	Assign	Cause	Bi-nih-nani	Cause
At	Ah-di	At	Cave	Tsa-ond	Rock cave
Attack	Al-tah-je-jay	Attack	Ceiling	Da-tel-jay	Seal
Attempt	Bo-o-ne-tah (a)	Try	Cemetary	Jish-cha	Among devils
Attention	Giha	Attention	Center	Ulh-ne-ih	Center
Authenticator	Hani-ba-ah-ho-zin	Know about	Change	Thla-go-a-nat-zah	Change
Authorize	Be-bo-ho-snee	Authorize			
Available	Ta-shoz-teh-ih	Available			
Baggage	Klailh (b)	Baggage			
Banzai	Ne-tah	Fool them			
Barge	Besh-na-elt	Barge			
Barrage	Besh-ba-wa-chind	Barrage			
Barrier	Bih-chan-ni-ah	In the way			
Base	Bih-tsee-dih	Base			
Battery	Bih-be-al-doh-tka-ih	Three guns			
Battle	Da-ah-hi-dzi-tsio	Battle	Channel	Ha-talhi-yazzie	Small singer
Bay	Toh-ah-hi-ghinh	Bay	Charge	Ah-tah-gi-jah	Charge
Bazooka	Ah-zhol	Bazooka	Chemical	Ta-nee	Alkali
Be	Tses-nah	Bee	Circle	Nas-pas	Circle
Beach	Tah-bahn (b)	Beach	Circuit	Ah-heh-ha-dailh	Circuit
Been	Tses-nah-nes-chee	Bee nut	Class	Alth-ah-a-teh	Class
Before	Bih-tse-dih	Before	Clear	Yo-ah-hol-zhod	Clear
Begin	Ha-hol-ziz	Commence from	Cliff	Tse-ye-chee	Cliff
Belong	Tses-nah-snez	Long bee	Close	Ul-chi-uh-nal-yah	Close
Between	Bi-tah-kiz	Between	Coast guard	Ta-bas-dsissi	Shore runner
Beyond	Bilh-la di	Down below	Code	Yil-tas	Peck
Bivouac	Ehl-nas-teh	Brush shelter	Colon	Naki-alh-deh-da-al-zhin	Two spots
Bomb	A-ye-shi	Eggs			
Booby trap	Dineh-ba-whoa-blehi	Man trap	Column	Alth-kay-ne-zih	Column
Borne	Ye-chie-tsah	Born elk	Combat	Da-ah-hi-jih-ganh	Fighting
Boundary	Ka-yah-bi-na-has-dzoh(b)	Boundary	Combination	Al-tkas-ei	Mixed
			Come	Huc-quo	Come
Bull dozer	Dola-alth-whosh	Bull sleep	Comma	Tsa-na-dahl	Tail drop
Bunker	Tsas-ka	Sandy hollow	Commercial	Nai-el-ne-hi	Commercial
But	Neh-dih	But	Commit	Huc-quo-la-jish	Come glove
By	Be-gha	By	Communication	Ha-neh-al-enji	Making talk
			Conceal	Be-ki-asz-jole	Conceal
			Concentration	Ta-la-hi-jih	One place
			Concussion	Whe-hus-dil	Concussion
			Condition	Ah-ho-tai	How it is
			Conference	Be-ke-ya-ti	Talk over
			Confidential	Na-nil-in	Kept secret

Corps: Clan

WORD	NAVAJO WORD	LITERAL TRANSLATION	WORD	NAVAJO WORD	LITERAL TRANSLATION
Confirm	Ta-a-neh	Make sure	Drive	Ah-nol-kahl	Drive
Conquer	A-keh-des-dlin	Won	Dud	Di-giss-yahzie	Small dummy
Consider	ne-tsa-cas	Think it over	Dummy	Di-giss-tso	Big dummy
Consist	bilh (c)	Consist			
Consolidate	Ah-hih-hi-nil	Put together	Each	Ta-lahi-ne-zini-go(d)	Each
Construct	Ahl-neh	To make	Echelon	Who-dzah	Line
Contact	aAh-hi-di-dail	Come together	Edge	Be-ba-hi	Edge
Continue	Ta-yi-teh	Continue	Effective	Be-delh-need	Effective
Control	Nai-ghiz	Control	Effort	Yea-go	With all your might
Convoy	Tkal-kah-o-nel	Moving on water	Element	Ah-na-nai	Troop representing
Coordinate	Beh-eh-ho-zin-	Known lines			others
	na-as-dzoh		Elevate	Ali-khi-ho-ne-oha	Elevate
Counter attack	Woltah-al-ki-gi-jeh	Counter act	Eliminate	Ha-beh-to-dzil	Eliminate
Course	Co-ji-goh	Course	Embark	Eh-ho-jay	Get on
Craft	ah-toh	Nest	Emergency	Ho-nez-cla	Emergency
Creek	Toh-nil-tsanh	Very little water	Emplacement	La-az-nil	Emplacement
Cross	Al-n-as-dzoh	Cross	Encircle	Ye-nas-teh (e)	Encircle
Cub	Shush-yahz	Cub	Encounter	Bi-khanh	Go against
			Engage	A-ha-ne-ho-ta	Agreed
Dash	Us-dzoh	Dash	Engine	Chidi-bi-tsi-t-	Engine
Dawn	Ha-yeli-kahn	Dawn		sine (e)	
Defense	Ah-kin-cil-toh	Defense	Engineer	Day-dil-jah-he	Engineer
Degree	Nahl-kihd	Degree	Enlarge	Nih-tsa-goh-al-neh	Make big
Delay	Be-sitihn	Deer lay	Enlist	Bih-zih-a-da-yi-lah	Enlist
Deliver	Be-bih-zihde	Deer liver	Entire	Ta-a-tah (e)	Entire
Demolition	Ah-deel-tahi	Blow up	Entrench	E-gad-ah-ne-lih	Make ditch
Dense	Ho-dilh-cla (d)	Wet	Envelop	A-zah-gi-ya	Envelop
Depart	Da-de-yah	Depart	Equipment	Ya-ha-de-tahi	Equipment
Department	Hogan	Department	Erect	Yeh-zihn	Stand up
Designate	Ye-khi-del-nei	Point out	Escape	A-zeh-ha-ge-yah	Escape
Desperate	Ah-da-ah-ho-dzah	Down to last	Establish	Has-tay-dzah	Establish
Detach	Al-cha-nil	Detached	Estimate	Bih-ke-tse-hod-	Estimate
Detail	Be-beh-sha	Deer tail		des-kez	
Detonator	Ah-deel-tahi (or)	Blown up	Evacuate	Ha-na	Evacuate
Difficult	Na-ne-klah	Difficult	Except	Neh-dih (e)	Except
Dig in	Le-eh-gade	Dig in	Except	Na-wol-ne	Expect
Direct	Ah-ji-go	Direct	Exchange	Alh-nahl-yah	Exchange
Disembark	Eh-ha-jay	Get out	Execute	A-do-nil	Execute
Dispatch	La-chai-en-seis-	Dog is patch	Explosive	Ah-del-tahi (e)	Explosive
	Be-jay		Expedite	Shil-loh (e)	Speed up
Displace	Hih-do-nal	Move	Extend	Ne-tdale	Make wide
Display	Be-seis-na-neh	Deer is play	Extreme	Al-tsan-ah-bahm	Each end
Disposition	A-ho-tey	Disposition			
Distribute	Nah-neh	Distribute	Fail	Cha-al-eind	Fail
District	Be-thin-ya-ni-che	Deer ice strict	Failure	Yees-ghin	Failure
Do	tse-le	Small pup	Farm	Mai-be-he-ahgan	Fox arm
Document	Beh-eh-ho-zinz	Document	Feed	Dzeh-chi-yon	Feed

Fortification: Cliff dwelling

WORD	NAVAJO WORD	LITERAL TRANSLATION	WORD	NAVAJO WORD	LITERAL TRANSLATION
Field	Clo-dih (f)	Field	Important	Ba-has-teh	Important
Fierce	Toh-bah-ha-zsid	Afraid	Improve	Ho-dol-zhond	Improve
File	Ba-eh-chez	File	Include	El-tsod	Include
Final	Tah-ah-kwo-dih	That is all	Increase	Ho-nalh	Increase
Flame thrower	Coh-ah-ghil-tlid	Flame thrower	Indicate	Ba-hal-neh	Tell about
Flank	Dah-di-kad	Flank	Infantry	Ta-neh-nal-dahi	Infantry
Flare	Wo-chi	Light streak	Infiltrate	Ye-gha-ne-jeh	Went through
Flight	Ma-e-as-zloli	Fox light	Initial	Beh-ed-de-dlid	Brand
Force	Ta-na-ne-ladi	Without care	Install	Ehd-tnah	Install
Form	Be-cha	Form	Installation	Nas-nil	In place
Formation	Be-cha-ye-lailh	Formation	Instruct	Na-ne-tgin	Teach
Fortification	Ah-na-sozi	Cliff dwelling	Intelligence	Ho-ya (i)	Smart
Fortify	Ah-na-sozi-yazzie	Small fortification	Intense	Dzeel	Strength
Forward	Tehi	Let's go	Intercept	Yel-na-me-jah	Intercept
Fragmentation	Besh-yazzie	Small metal	Interfere	Ah-nilh-khlai	Interfere
Frequency	Ha-talhi-tso	Big singer	Interpret	Ah-tah-ha-ne	Interpret
Friendly	Neh-hecho-da-ne	Friendly	Investigate	Na-ali-ka	Track
From	Bi-tsan-dehn	From	Involve	A-tah	Involve
Furnish	Yeas-nil (f)	Furnish	Is	Seis	Seven
Further	Wo-nas-di	Further	Island	Seis-keyah	Seven island
			Isolate	Bih-tsa-nel-kad	Separate
Garrison	Yah-a-da-hal-yon-ih	Take care of			
Gasoline	Chidi-bi-toh	Gasoline	Jungle	Woh-di-chil	Jungle
Grenade	Ni-ma-si	Potatoes			
Guard	Ni-dih-da-hi	Guard	Kill	Naz-tsaid	Kill
Guide	Nah-e-thlai	Guide	Kilocycle	nas-tsaid-a-kha-ah-yeh-ha-dilh	Kill oil go around

Grenade: Potatoes

WORD	NAVAJO WORD	LITERAL TRANSLATION	WORD	NAVAJO WORD	LITERAL TRANSLATION
Hall	Lhi-ta-a-ta	Horse all	Labor	Na-nish (l)	Labor
Half track	Tlh-nih-jah-a-quhe	Race track	Land	Kay-yah	Land
Halt	Ta-akwai-i	Halt	Launch	Tka-ghil-zhod	Launch
Handle	Bet-seen	Handle	Leader	Ah-na-ghai	Leader
Have	Jo	Have	Least	De-be-yazie-ha-a-ah	Lamb feast
Headquarter	Na-ha-tah-ta-ba-hogan	Headquarter	Leave	Dah-de-yah	He left
Held	Wo-tah-ta-eh-dahn-oh	Held (past tense)	Left	Nish-cla-jih-goh	Left
High	Wo-tah	High	Less	Bi-oh (l)	Less
High explosive	Be-al-doh-be-ca-bih-dzil-igi	Powerful shell	Level	Dil-konh	Level
			Liaison	Da-a-he-gi-eneh	Know other's action
Highway	Wo-tah-ho-ne-teh	High way	Limit	Ba-has-ah	Limit
Hold	Wo-tkanh	Hold	Litter	Ni-das-ton (l)	Scatter
Hospital	A-zey-al-ih	Place of medicine	Locate	A-kwe-eh	Spot
Hostile	A-nah-ne-dzin	Not friendly	Loss	Ut-din	Loss
Howitzer	Be-el-don-ts-quodi	Short big gun			
			Machine gun	A-knah-as-donih	Rapid fire gun
Illuminate	Wo-chi (i)	Light up	Magnetic	Na-e-lahi	Pick up
Immediately	Shil-loh (i)	Immediately	Manage	Hastni-beh-na-hai	Man age
Impact	A-he-dis-goh	Impact	Maneuver	Na-na-o-nalth	Moving around
			Map	Kah-ya-nesh-chai	Map
			Maximum	Bel-dil-khon	Fill to top

120

WORD	NAVAJO WORD	LITERAL TRANSLATION	WORD	NAVAJO WORD	LITERAL TRANSLATION
Mechanic	Chiti-a-nayl-inih	Auto repairman	Or	Eh-do-dah-goh	Either
Mechanized	Chidi-da-ah-he-goni	Fighting cars	Orange	Tchil-lhe-soi	Orange
Medical	A-zay	Medicine	Order	Be-eh-ho-zini	Order
Megacycle	Mil-ah-heh-ah-dilh	Million go around	Ordnance	Lei-az-jah	Under ground
Merchant ship	Na-el-nehi-tsin-na-ailh	Merchant ship	Originate	Das-teh-do	Begin
			Other	La-e-cih	Other
Message	Hane-al-neh	Message	Out	Clo-dih	Out side
Military	Silago-keh-goh	Military	Overlay	Be-ka-has-tsoz	Overlay
Millimeter	Na-as-tso-si-a-ye-do-tish	Double mouse			
			Parenthesis	Atsanh	Rib
Mine	Ha-gade	Mine	Particular	A-yo-ad-do-neh	Particular
Minimum	Be-oh (m)	Minimum	Party	Da-sha-jah	Party
Minute	Ah-khay-el-kit-yazzie	Little hour	Pay	Na-eli-ya	Pay
			Penalize	Tah-ni-des-tanh	Set back
Mission	Al-neshodi	Mission	Percent	Yal	Money
Mistake	O-zhi	Miss	Period	da-ahl-zhin	Period
Mopping	Ha-tao-di	Mopping	Periodic	da-al-zhin-thin-moasi	Period ice cat
More	Thla-na-nah	More			
Mortar	Be-al-doh-cid-da-hi	Sitting gun	Permit	Gos-shi-e	Permit
Motion	Na-hot-nah	Motion	Personnel	Da-ne-lei	Member
Motor	Chide-be-tse-tsen	Car head	Photograph	Beh-chi-ma-had-nil	Photograph
			Pill box	bi-so-dih-dot-sahi-bi-tsahsick	Pig box
Native	Ka-ha-teni	Native			
Navy	Tal-kah-silago	Sea soldier	Pinned down	Bil-dah-has-tanh-ya	Pinned down
Necessary	Ye-na-zehn	Want	Plane	Tsidi	bird
Negative	Do-ya-sho-da	No good	Plasma	Dil-di-ghili	Plasma
Net	Na-nes-dizi	Net	Point	Be-so-de-dez-ahe	Pig point
Neutral	Do-neh-lini	Neutral	Pontoon	Tkosh-jah-da-na-elt	Floating barrel
Normal	Doh-a-ta-h-dah	Normal	Position	bilh-has-ahn	Position
Not	Ni-dah-than-zie	No turkey	Possible	Ta-ha-ah-tay	Possible
Notice	Ne-da-tazi-thin	No turkey ice	Post	Sah-dei	Post
Now	Kut	Now	Prepare	Hash-tay-ho-dit-ne	Prepare
Number	Neh-bih-ke-as-chinigh	What's written	Present	Kut	Present
			Previous	Bih-tse-dih	Previous
			Primary	Altseh-nan-day-hi-gih	1st postion
Objective	Bi-ne-yei	Goal			
Observe	Hal-zid	Observe	Priority	Hane-pesodi	Priority
Obstacle	Da-ho-desh-zha	Obstacle	Probable	Da-tsi	Probable
Occupy	Yeel-tsod	Taken	Problem	Na-nish-tsoh	Big job
Of	Toh-ni-tkal-lo	Ocean fish	Proceed	Nay-nih-jih	Go
Offensive	Bin-kie-jinh-jih-dez-jay	Offensive	Progress	Nah-sai	Progress
			Protect	Ah-chanh	Self defense
Once	Ta-lai-di	Once	Provide	Yis-nil	Provide
Only	Ta-ei-tay-a-yah	Only	Purple	Dinl-chi	Purple
Operate	Ye-nahl-nish	Work at	Pyrotechnic	Coh-na-chanh	Pancy fire
Opportunity	Ash-ga-alin	Opportunity			
Opposition	Ne-he-tsah-jih-shin	Opposition	Question	Ah-jah	Ear

Pyrotechnic: Fancy fire

WORD	NAVAJO WORD	LITERAL TRANSLATION	WORD	NAVAJO WORD	LITERAL TRANSLATION
Quick	Shil-loh	Quick	Route	Gah-bih-tkeen	Rabbit trail
Radar	Esat-tsanh (r)	Listen	Runner	Nih-dzid-teih	Runner
Raid	Dezjay	Raid			
Railhead	A-de-geh-hi	Hipping point	Sabotage	A-tkel-yah	Hindered
Railroad	Konh-na-al-bansi-bi-thin	Railroad	Saboteur	A-tkel-el-ini	Trouble maker
			Sailor	Cha-le-gai	White caps
Rallying	A-lah-na-o-glalih	Gathering	Salvage	Na-has-glah	Pick them up
Range	An-zah	Distance	Sat	Bih-la-sana-cid-da-hi	Apple sitting
Rate	Gah-eh-yahn	Rabbit ate			
Ration	Na-a-jah	Ration	Scarlet, red	Lhe-chi (s & r)	Red
Ravine	Chush-ka (r)	Ravine	Schedule	Beh-eh-ho-zini	Schedule
Reach	Il-day (r)	Reach	Scout	Ha-a-sid-al-sizi-gih	Short racoon
Ready	Kut (r)	Ready			
Rear	Be-ka-denh (r)	Rear	Screen	Besh-na-nes-dizi	Screen
Receipt	Shoz-teh	Receipt	Seaman	Tkal-kah-dineh-ih	Seaman
Recommend	Che-ho-tai-tahn	Recommend	Secret	Bah-has-tkih	Secret
Reconnaissance	Ha-a-cidi	Inspector	Sector	yoehi (s)	Sector
Reconnoiter	Ta-ha-ne-al-ya	Make sure	Secure	ye-dzhe-al-tsisi	Small security
Record	Gah-ah-nah-kloli	R-e-rope	Seize	yeel-stod	Seize
Red	Li-chi	Red	Select	be-tah-has-gla	Took out
Reef	Tsa-zhin	Black rock	Semi colon	Da-ahl-zhin-bi-tsa-na-dahl	Dot drop
Reembark	Eh-na-coh	Go in			
Refire	Na-na-coh	Refire	Set	Dzeh-cid-da-hi	Elk sitting
Regulate	Na-yel-n	Regulate	Shackle	Di-bah-nesh-gohz	Shackle
Reinforce	Nal-dzil	Reinforce	Shell	Be-al-doh-be-ca	Shell
Relief	Aganh-tol-jay	Relief	Shore	Tah-bahn (s)	Shore
Relieve	Nah-jih-co-nal-ya	Remove	Short	Bosh-keesh	Short
Reorganize	Ha-dit-zah	Reorganize	Side	Bosh-keesh	Side
Replacement	Ni-na-do-nil	Replacement	Sight	Ye-el-tsanh	Seen
Report	Who-neh	Got word	Signal	Na-eh-eh-gish	By signs
Representative	Tka-naz-nili	Triple men	Simplex	Alah-ih-ne-tih	Inner wire
Request	jo-kayed-goh	Ask for	Sit	Tkin-cid-da-hi	Ice sitting
Reserve	Hesh-j-e	Reserve	Situate	A-ho-tay (s)	Situate
Restrict	Ba-ho-chini	Restrict	Smoke	Lit	Smoke
Retire	Ah-hos-teend	Retire	Sniper	Oh-behi	Pick 'em off
Retreat	Ji-din-nes-chanh	Retreat	Space	Be-tkah	Between
Return	Na-dzah	Came back	Special	E-yih-sih	Main thing
Reveal	Who-neh (l)	Reveal	Speed	Yo-zons	Swift motion
Revert	Na-si-yiz	Turn about	Sporadic	Ah-na-ho-neil	Now and then
Revetment	Ba-nas-cla (r)	Corner	Spotter	Eel-tsay-i	Spotter
Ridge	Gah-ghil-keid	Rabbit ridge	Spray	Klesh-so-dilzin	Snake pray
Rifleman	Be-al-do-hosteen	Riflemen	Squadron	Nah-ghizi	Squash
River	Toh-yil-kal	Much water	Storm	Ne-ol	Storm
Robot bomb	A-ye-shi-na-tah-ih	Egg fly	Straff	Na-wo-ghi-goid	Hoe
Rocket	Lesz-yil-beshi	Sand boil	Straggler	Chy-ne-de-dahe	Straggler
Roll	Yeh-mas	Roll	Strategy	Na-ha-tah (s)	Strategy
Round	Naz-pas (r)	Round	Stream	Toh-ni-lih	Running water

Submarine: Iron fish

WORD	NAVAJO WORD	LITERAL TRANSLATION
Strength	Dzhel	Strength
Stretch	Desz-tsood	Stretch
Strike	Nay-dal-ghal	Strike
Strip	Ha-tih-jah	Strip
Stubborn	nil-ta	Stubborn
Subject	na-nish-yazzie	Small job
Submerge	tkal-cla-yi-yah	Went under water
Submit	A-nih-leh	Send
Subordinate	Al-khi-nal-dzl	Helping each other
Succeed	Yah-tay-go-e-elah	Make good
Success	Ut-zah	It is done
Successful	Ut-zah-ha-dez-bin	It is done well
Successive	Ut-zah-sid	Success scar
Such	Yis-cleh	Sox
Suffer	to-ho-ne	Suffer
Summary	Shin-go-bah	Summer mary
Supplementary	Tka-go-ne-nan-dey-he	3rd position
Supply	Nal-yeh-hi	Supply
Supply ship	Nalga-hi-tsin-nah-ailh	Supply ship
Support	Ba-ah-hot-gli	Depend
Surrender	Ne-na-cha	Surrender
Surround	Naz-pas (s)	Surround
Survive	Yis-da-ya	Survive
System	di-ba-tsa-as-zhi-bi-tsin	System
Tactical	E-chihn	Tactical
Take	Gah-tahn	Take
Tank	Chay-da-gahi	Tortoise

Tank: Tortoise

WORD	NAVAJO WORD	LITERAL TRANSLATION
Tank destroyer	Chay-da-gahi-nail-tsaidi	Tortoise killer
Target	Wol-doni	Target
Task	Tazi-na-eh-dil-kid	Turkey ask
Team	Deh-na-as-tso-si	Tea mouse
Terrace	Ali-khi-ho-ne-oha(t)	Terrace
Terrain	Tashi-na-hal-thin	Turkey rain
Territory	Ka-yah (t)	Territory
That	Tazi-cha	Turkey hat
The	Cha-gee	Blue-jay
Their	Bih	Their
Thereafter	Ta-zi-kwa-i-be-ka-di	Turkey here after
These	Cha-gi-o-eh	The see
They	Cha-gee (y)	The y
This	Di	The

WORD	NAVAJO WORD	LITERAL TRANSLATION
Together	Ta-bilh	Together
Torpedo	Lo-be-ca	Fish shell
Total	Ta-al-so	Total
Tracer	Beh-na-al-kah-hi	Tracer
Traffic diagram	Hane-ba-na-as-dzoh	Diagram story line
Train	Coh-nai-ali-bahn-si	Train
Transportation	A-hah-da-a-cha	Transportation
Trench	T-gade	Trench
Triple	Tka-ih	Triple
Troop	Nal-deh-hi	Troop
Truck	Chido-tso	Big auto
Type	Alth-ah-a-teh	Type
Under	bi-yah	Under
Unidentified	Do-bay-hosen-e	Unidentified
Unit	Da-az-jah (u)	Unit
Unshackle	No-da-eh-nesh-gohz	Unshackle
Until	Uh-quo-ho	Until
Vicinity	Na-hos-ah-gih	There about
Village	Chah-ho-oh-lhan-ih	Many shelter
Visibility	Nay-es-tee	Visibility
Vital	Ta-eh-ye-sy	Vital
Warning	Bilh-he-neh (w)	Warning
Was	Ne-teh	Was
Water	Tkoh	Water
Wave	Vilh-kolh	Wave
Weapon	Beh-dah-a-hi-jih-gani	Fighting weapon
Well	To-ha-ha-dlay	Well
When	Gloe-eh-na-ah-wo-hai	Weasel hen
Where	Gloe-ih-qui-ah	Weasel here
Which	Gloe-ih-a-hsi-tlon	Weasel tied together
Will	Gloe-ih-dot-sahi	Sick weasel
Wire	Besh-tsosie	Small wire
With	Bilh (w)	With
Within	Bilh-bigih	With in
Without	Ta-gaid	Without
Wood	Chiz	Fire wood
Wound	Cah-da-khi	Wound
Yard	A-del-tahl	Yard
Zone	Bih-na-has-dzoh	Zone

SOURCE: *Department of the Navy—Naval Historical Center. Revised as of June 15, 1945; declassified under Department of Defense directive 5200.9.*

Metro-Goldwyn-Mayer Pictures *Presents*

A Lion Rock Production

A John Woo Film
WINDTALKERS

Casting by . . . . Mindy Marin, C.S.A.
Music Composed and Conducted by . . . . James Horner
Co-Producers . . . . Caroline Macaulay, Arthur Anderson
Edited by . . . . .Steven Kemper, Jeff Gullo and Tom Rolf, A.C.E.
Production Designer . . . . Holger Gross
Director of Photography . . . . Jeffrey Kimball, A.S.C.
Line Producers . . . . John J. Smith, Richard Stenta
Executive Producer . . . . C.O. Erickson
Produced by .John Woo, Terence Chang,
Tracie Graham, Alison Rosenzweig
Written by . . . . John Rice & Joe Batteer
Directed by . . . . .John Woo

CAST

Joe Enders . . . . Nicolas Cage
Ben Yahzee . . . . Adam Beach
Charlie Whitehorse . . . . Roger Willie
Ox Henderson . . . . Christian Slater
Hjelmstad . . . . Peter Stormare
Chick . . . . Noah Emmerich
Fortino . . . . William Morts
Pappas . . . . Mark Ruffalo
Nellie . . . . Martin Henderson
Harrigan . . . . Brian Van Holt
Rita . . . . Frances O'Connor
Ear Doctor . . . . Kevin Cooney
Camp Tarawa Staff Sargeant . . . . Scott Atkinson
Major Mellitz . . . . Jason Isaacs
Marine . . . . Jeremy Davidson
Colonel Hollings . . . . Holmes Osborne
Kittring . . . . Keith Campbell
Hasby . . . . Clayton Barber
Mertens . . . . Cameron Thor
Corpsman . . . . Brian F. Maynard
Japanese Intelligence Officer . . . . Brian Kasai
Japanese Radio Operator . . . . Hiroshi "Rosh" Mori
Japanese Bunker Commander . . . . John Takeshi Ichikawa
Eddie the Bartender . . . . .Ross Lasi Tanoai
Japanese Bunker Gunner . . . . Christopher T. Yamamoto
Marine Artillery Commander . . . . Marc McClellan
Japanese Artillery Officer . . . . Steve Tanizaki
Field Hospital Colonel . . . . James Dever

Charan Kanoa Boy . . . . Aaron Yamagata
N.C.O. Officer . . . . Jon Michael Souza
Charan Kanoa Girl . . . . Carissa Jung
Charan Kanoa Mother . . . . Victoria Chen
Japanese Artillery . . . . Wataru Yoshida
Japanese Artillery Sighter . . . . Junya Oishi
Japanese Artillery Gunner . . . . Jiro Koga
Navajo Man . . . . Albert Smith
Navajo Instructor . . . . Vincent Whipple
Marine Recruit . . . . Jim Morse
Battleship Codetalker . . . . Malcolm Dohi
Battleship Petty Office . . . . Darrel Guilbeau
Sgt. Code Instructor . . . . Chris Devlin
Tech Sgt. . . . . Jeff Davis
Radio Codetalker . . . . Glen Begay
Hula Dancers . . . . Lynn Kawailele Allen
Tina Leialoha Gube, Alewa T. Olotoa,
Ilima Pumphrey, Lena Savaiinaea, Kaliko Scott

Stunt Coordinator . . . . Brian Smrz
Stunt Co-Coordinators . . . . Gregg Smrz
Eddie Yansick
Al Goto
Helicopter Pilot . . . . Cliff Fleming
Pilots . . . . Craig Hosking
Robert S. Hosking
Stunt Players . . . . Tsuyoshi Abe, Charles K. Aleka,
Kenny Alexander, Chris Antonucci, John Ashker,
Greg Barnett, David Barrett, Paul Beahm, Joey Box,
John Branagan, Bobbie Brown, Troy Brown,
Richard Bucher, Bobby Burns, John Cade,
Christopher Caso, Mark Chadwick,Doc Charbonneau,
Eric Chen, Arnold Chon, Phil Culatta, Craig Davis,
Tim Davison, Stephan DeRelian, Paul Eliopoulos,
Masa Endo, Jonathan Eusebio, Roel Failma,
Dane Farwell, Edward Fernandez, Colin Fong,
Robert "Rock" Galotti, Dale Gibson, Tim Gilbert,
Tanner Gill, Dong Quan Ha, Shane Habberstad,
Randy Hall Steven Ho, Zach Hudson, Yoshio Ilzuka,
Brian Imada, Steven Ito, Terry Jackson, Keii Johnston,
Brett Jones, Kim Kahana, Jr., Jon W. Kishi, Hiro Koda,
Kim Koscki, John Koyama, Peter Lai, Dan Lemieux,
Will Leong, Michael Li, Clint Lilley, Juddson Linn,
Brock Little, Johnny Martin, Steven Martinez,
Dustin Meier, Edward K. Mook, Hien Nguyen,
Chris O'Hara, Carrick O'Quinn, Vladimir Orlov,
Michael P. Owen, Chad Parker, Denney Pierce,
Casey Pieretti, Stuart Quan, Rex J. Reddick,
Simon Rhee, Maro-uo Richmond, Shawn Robinson,

David Rowden, Mike Rufino, Jon Sakata,
Spencer Sano, Myke Schwartz, Paul Short,
Gunter Simon, Brian Simpson, Erik Stabenau,
Mark Stefanich, Jim Stephan, Philip Tan, Frank Torres,
Gary Toy, Michael Trisler, Jon Valera, Jose Vasquez
Lee Waddell, David Wald, Scott Waugh, Alex Wen,
Lee Whittaker, Brian J. Williams, Thomas E. Williams,
Danny Wong, Scott Workman, Marcus Young, Ron Yuan

Production Manager	John J. Smith
First Assistant Director	Arthur Anderson
Second Assistant Director	Joan Cunningham
Special Make-up Effects Created by	Kevin Yagher
Supervising Sound Editor	Mark Stoeckinger
Re-Recording Sound Mixers	David Fluhr
	Randy Thom
Visual Effects Supervisor	Kevin Lingenfelser
Visual Effects Producer	Kevin Elam
Associate Producer/Production Supervisor	Steve Traxler
Art Director	Kevin Ishioka
Set Decorator	Richard Goodard
Assistant Art Director	Maya Shimoguchi
Camera Operator	Greg Lundsgaard
First Assistant Camera	Ken Nishino
Second Assistant Camera	Dale White
Loader	Lynda Wu
"B" Camera Operator	Michael St. Hilaire
First Assistant "B" Camera	Dennis Seawright
Second Assistant "B" Camera	Vince Mata
"C" Camera Operator	Jeff Mart
First Assistant "C" Camera	Zoran Veselic
Second Assistant "C" Camera	Don Steinberg
"D" Camera Operator	Leo Napolitano
First Assistant "D" Camera	Gregory Irwin
Second Assistant "D" Operator	Shawn Landis
Camera Technician	Jian Cong
Steadicam Operators	Greg Lundsgaard
	Mark Van Loon
Still Photographer	Stephen Vaughan
Video Assist Operators	Jeb Johenning
	John Trunk
Script Supervisor	Cate Hardman
Production Coordinators	Gary MacPherson
	Devon Dibble
Accountant	Marilyn Tasso
Chief Lighting Technician	Dan Delgado
Assistant Lighting Technician	Frank Mathews
Rigging Chief Lighting Technician	Greg Langham
Rigging Assistant Lighting Technician	Jim Rose
Key Grip	Mike Popovich
Second Company Grip	Ray Chase
Dolly Grip	Tom Ruffner
	Mark Meyers
Key Rigging Grip	Tom Gibson
Rigging Grip Best Boy	Jerry Sandager
Technocrane Operator	Brian McPherson
Technocrane Assistant	Jim Favazzo
Locations Manager - Hawaii	Ginger Peterson
Locations Manager - Los Angeles	Kenneth Fix
Assistant Locations Manager - Hawaii	Daniel Wainrib
Assistant Locations Manager - Los Angeles	Stephen Fischer
Additional Second Assistant Directors	Jeff Bilger
	Alison Troy
Second Second Assistant Director	Randol Perelman-Taylor
First Assistant Editor	Raymond Boniker
Second Assistant Editor	Tony Chiu
Avid Editor	Janet Ogletree
Visual Effects Editor	Clark Campbell
Projectionist	Walter McCormick
Production Sound Mixer	Richard Goodman
Boom Operator	Joel Shryack
Cable	Tom Giordano
Additional Sound Mixer	Lee Alexander
Temp Music Editors	Dick Bernstein
	Philip Tallman
Costume Supervisor	Nick Scarano
Key Costumer	Anthony Scarano
Key Military Costumer	Richard Schoen
Costumers	Jorge Gonzalez
	Brian Callahan
Key Make-up	Steve LaPorte
Make-up	Mark Landon
	Bill Myer
Nicolas Cage's Make-up	Allen Weisinger
Additional Make-up	Maggie Myer
Special Effects Make-up Supervisor	Mitch Coughlin
Special Effects Key Make-up	Rick Stratton
Special Effects Make-up	Jamie Kelman
Body Effects	Fred Cervantes
Key Hair Stylist	Janis Clark
Hair Stylists	Linda Leiter-Sharp
	Linda Rizzuto
Wig Maker	Carol Doran
Nicolas Cage's Hair Stylists	William Farley
	Joseph Coscia
Property Master	Don Miloyevich

Assistant Property Master	Michael Hansen
Property Assistants	Chris Langevin
	Kris Peck
	Michael Driscoll
Art Department Coordinators	Lynette Wich
	Abigail Sheiner
Lead Man	John Schacht
Set Dresser	Glenn Roberts
WWII Research	Debra Silverman
Construction Coordinator	Gary Deaton
Construction General Foreman	Bill Boyd
Construction Accountant	Janine McEuen
Paint Foreman	George Hanson
Standby Painter	Cliff Berns
Greens Person	Craig Ayers
Lead Set Designer	A. Todd Holland
Set Designer	Luis G. Hoyos
Special Effects Coordinator	Phil Cory
Special Effects Co-Coordinator	Dave Simmons
Special Effects Supervisors	John Frazier
	Jan H. Aaris
Special Effects Set Coordinator	John McLeod
Special Effects Foreman	Mike Edmondson
	Richard Cory
Special Effects Purchaser	Steven Riley
Special Effects Accountants	Bryan Yaconelli
	Sharon Segal
Transportation Coordinator	Ed Arter
Transportation Captain	LeRoy Reed
Transportation Co-Captain	Beau Reed
Transportation Dispatcher - Hawaii	Linda Wojcieski
Transportation Dispatcher - Los Angeles	Tina Arter-Duquette
Unit Publicist	Bronwyn Preston
Assistant Production Coordinator	Jennifer Webb
Assistant Accountants	Joene Acord
	Gavin Behrman
	Lamonte Bell
	Taffy Schweickhardt
	Anthea Strangis
	Elpe Villard
Accounting Clerk	Arlette Yaconelli
Production Secretary	Jana Lundy
Assistants to Terence Chang	Lai Yee Ng
	Todd Weinger
Assistant to John Woo	Ashley Fondrevay
Personal Assistant to John Woo	Casey Collins
Casting Associate	Amanda Harding
Extras Casting	Tammy L. Smith
Extras Casting Coordinator	Dixie Webster-Davis

DGA Trainee	Mark Rabinowitz
Key Set PA	Todd Skaggs
Production Assistants	Mark C. Smith,
	Noah Cooksey, Frederick Shear,
	Brice Potthoff, Jr., Danny Mormino,
	Mike Gillis, Scott Kirkley,
	Steve Simon, Joyce Green,
	Amy Wilkins, Nalani Blane,
	Kiana Awong, Brook Fain,
	Thomas Healy, Jon McBride
Video Production Assistant	Luciano Blotta
Post Production Assistant	John Quinn
Catering	Tony's Food Service
Craft Service - Hawaii	Donovan Ahuna
Craft Service - Los Angeles	Michael Starks
Medical Coordinator	Brian Maynard
Medics	Robert Allen, David Falicki,
	Chris Carrington, Mark Yeager
Security	Reno Domenik & Associates
Nicolas Cage's Stand-in	Marco Kyris
Military Advisor	James Dever
Department of Defense	
Project Officer	Captain Matt Morgan, USMC
Japanese Military Advisor	Dan King
Military Historian	Tom Williams
Artillery Coordinator	Mike Gibbons
Artillery Advisors	Rick Pohlers
	Bill Guiette
Navajo Code Talker Advisor	Albert Smith
Navajo Advisor	Richard Begay

Second Unit

Second Unit Directed by	Brian Smrz
First Assistant Director	Joan Cunningham

KEVIN YAGHER PRODUCTIONS INC.
Crew

Project Supervisor	Mitch Coughlin
Studio Coordinator	Bryan Sides
Painters	Chris Hanson
	James Hogue
Sculptor	Eli Romaire
Mold/Lab Technicians	Fred Cervantes,
	David Selvadurai, John Halfmann,
	Shownee Smith, Nevada Smith,
	Tim Jarvis, Jamie Kelman,
	Mark Sisson, Michael Wickerham

Body Fabrication . . . . Karen Mason
Rick Cedillo
Mechanical Technicians . . . . Johnnie Spence
David Miner
Hair Technicians . . . . Robert Phillips
Rufus Hearn
Production Assistant . . . . James Patterson
Studio/Contract Advisor . . . . Mark C. Yagher

Visual Effects and Animation by Cinesite

CG Supervisor . . . . David T. Altenau
CG Modeler/Animator . . . . Lynn Basas
CG Texture Painter . . . . Brian Ripley
CG Animator . . . . Cliff Mueller
CG Animator/Lighter . . . . David Satchwell
CG Lighter . . . . Darren Kiner
CG TD . . . . Irving Moy
Composite Supervisor . . . . Jerry Sells
Digital Compositors . . . . Kama Moiha
David Lingenfelser
Motion Tracking Supervisor . . . . Jeffrey Edward Baksinski
Motion Trackers . . . . Michael A. Ramirez
Arthur Sutherland
Anthony Serenil
Inferno Artist . . . . Joni Jacobson
VFX Coordinator . . . . Bridgitte Nance
VFX Editor . . . . Kevin Clark
Digital Asset Manager . . . . Vince Lavares
Data Operators . . . . Tony Sgueglia
Digital Imaging Technician . . . . Glen Gustafson

Animal action was monitored by the American Humane
Association. No animal was harmed in the making of this film.
Prosthetic animals were used in some scenes.

THE PRODUCERS WISH TO THANK:
National Baseball Hall Of Fame Library

Magazines provided by The Mainichi Newspapers

World War II-era Hershey Milk Chocolate bar labels courtesy
of Hershey Community Archives, Hershey, PA

Filmed in part on location at Kualoa Ranch and
Dillingham Estate Island of Oahu, Hawaii

SPACECAM Aerial Camera System provided by
SPACECAM SYSTEMS, INC.

GYROSPHERE® Aerial Camera System
provided by Flying Pictures USA

Titles and Opticals by . . . . Howard Anderson Company
Optical Sound Negative by . . . . N.T. Audio
Negative Cutter . . . . Gary Burritt
DTS Consultant . . . . John Keating

Recorded at Sony Studios

Avids by Eagle Eye Digital Film

Digital Storage by Archion

All Terrain Aerial Crane by U.F.O.

Camera Cranes by Chapman/Leonard Studio Equipment, Inc.

Visit the MGM Website at: www.mgm.com

The events, characters and firms depicted in this motion
picture are fictitious. Any similarity to actual persons, living
or dead, or to actual firms is purely coincidental.

DISTRIBUTED BY MGM DISTRIBUTION CO.

Acknowledgments

Newmarket Press expresses special thanks to the following for their special contributions to this book:

Metro-Goldwyn-Mayer Studios; Senator Jeff Bingaman for his introduction, expertise and all of his work on behalf of honoring the Navajo code talkers; Dana Krupa of Senator Jeff Bingaman's office; Laurence Walsh of John Woo's office; Laine Sutherland of Northern Arizona University's Cline Library Special Collections and Archives department for providing historical photographs of the Navajo; Katherine Flaherty of the National Archives and Records Administration for her assistance with photographs; and Lena Kaljot of the Marine Corps Historical Center for providing official photographs. Editor Antonia Felix and designer Timothy Shaner for their unflagging dedication to a project they both admire.

Unit photographer Stephen Vaughan for his magnificent photographs of the production.

Esther Margolis, Keith Hollaman, Shannon Berning, Frank DeMaio, Tom Perry, and Kelli Taylor at Newmarket Press.

Credits & Permissions

Senator Jeff Bingaman: pages 18, 46, 49, 114-115.

Marine Corps Historical Center: pages 19 (USMC#129851), 23 (USMC#82619), 24, 27 (USMC#69889-A), 28 (USMC#57875), 33 (USMC#117725), 34 (USMC#89670).

National Archives and Records Administration: pages 20 (USMC#124944), 26 (USMC#94236), 40-41 (NWDNS-208-N-29695), 42-43 (NWDNS-127-N-83261), 48 (USMC#69896).

Philip Johnston Collection, Cline Library, Northern Arizona University: pages 30-31, 50, 53, 54-55, 56-57, 77.

HASBRO and G.I. JOE are trademarks of Hasbro and used with permission. © 2001 Hasbro. All rights reserved. Page 35.

Kenji Kawano and Northland Publishing: Permission to reprint extracts of text and photographs from *Warriors: Navajo Code Talkers*, by Kenji Kawano © 1990 Kenji Kawano: pages 36-39.

The Gallup Independent, Jeffrey Jones: page 115.

Excerpts from *Navajo Code Talkers*, by Doris Paul, copyright 1973 by Doris Paul. Reprinted by permission of Dorrance Publishing Co., Inc.: pages 29, 31, 32, 35, 42.

Text excerpt on page 40 from the essay "WWII: Marines in the Mariana Islands," by Lyn Krukal, courtesy U.S. Marine Corps Historical Center.

Windtalkers Original Motion Picture Soundtrack, with music by Academy Award Winning composer James Horner, available on

RCAVICTOR

Suggested Reading

Downs, James F. *The Navajo*. Prospect Heights, Illinois: Waveland Press, 1984.

Durrett, Deanne. *Unsung Heroes of World War II: The Story of the Navajo Code Talkers*. New York: Facts on File, 1998.

Iverson, Peter. *The Navajos*. New York, Chelsea House, 1990.

Kawano, Kenji (photographer). *Warriors: Navajo Code Talkers*. Flagstaff: Northland Publishing, 1990.

McClain, Sally. *Navajo Weapon: The Navajo Code Talkers*. Tucson, Arizona: Rio Nuevo Publishers, 2002.

Paul, Doris Atkinson. *The Navajo Code Talkers*. Philadelphia: Dorance, 1973.

Simonelli, Jeanne M. *Crossing Between Worlds: The Navajos of Canyon de Chelly*. Santa Fe: SAR Press, 1997.

Web Sites

Senator Jeff Bingaman's Code Talkers page: bingaman.senate.gov/code_talkers

Harrison Lapahie, Jr.'s, Navajo Code Talkers page: www.lapahie.com/NavajoCodeTalker.cfm

The entire Navajo Code Talkers Dictionary: www.history.navy.mil/faqs/faq61-4.htm